W9-CEN-548

NOTE
INVESTING
MADE EASIER

HOW TO BUY & PROFIT FROM
DISTRESSED MORTGAGES

MARTIN SAENZ MBA MS

POWER
HOUSE
PUBLISHING

ALEXANDRIA
VIRGINIA

Note Investing Made Easier

How to buy and profit from distressed mortgages

by Martin Saenz

Published by:

Powerhouse Publishing

625 N. Washington Street, Suite 425

Alexandria, Virginia 22314

info@powerhousepublishing.net

703-982-0984

ISBN First Paperback Edition: 1546664319

Second paperback printing July 2017

Printed in the United States of America

Saenz, Martin

Note investing made easier, how to buy and profit from distressed mortgages

1st paperback ed.

ISBN-10: 1546664319

ISBN-13: 9781546664314

TABLE OF CONTENTS

CASE STUDIES

DEDICATION

I want to thank my mother and family for instilling in me the notion that I could do and be anything I wanted to be. And to my wife, Ruth, and 4 children, Joshua, Zachary, Emily, and Elijah, you are my true love and blessing in life.

ACKNOWLEDGEMENTS

I would like to express my gratitude to some of the folks whose professional advice and encouragement led to my growth and success in the note industry and inspired me to write this book.

I have to start with Marty Granoff. In 2013, my first experience in the note industry came as a customer selling a performing note to Marty Granoff. I learned a great deal about extensive due diligence and above and beyond risk mitigation techniques through that experience.

To Bill McCafferty, thank you for your more-than-generous advice throughout the years. The note business is not for the weak and timid. I consider you a good friend.

Added to that list are the players in the East Coast group: Deepta Hiremath, Paper Assets Capital Team, Fuquan Bilal, Yvonne Harper, Victoria Varrasse, Andrew McDannels, Ricky Brava, and the list goes on. I truly enjoy going to the meetups and learning as much as possible while sharing experiences.

ABOUT THE AUTHOR

Martin Saenz lives in Northern Virginia with his wife and four children. He formed a very successful Museum Exhibit company in 2006 that provided services to the Federal Government, which he sold in 2013.

He and his wife have been investing in residential and commercial real estate since 2009 and began investing in mortgage notes in 2013. Today he is the managing member of 2nd Chance Funding, LLC, a note investment company.

His portfolio of 1st and 2nd mortgage notes is spread out throughout the nation, and his residential & commercial property portfolio is held in the Washington DC area.

Martin holds an MBA from Drexel University and an M.S. in Project Management from George Washington University.

DISCLAIMER

Buying discounted notes is an industry that has been around for decades, and many banks, hedge funds, and other financial institutions take advantage of these types of opportunities. Sometimes they make money and sometimes they lose money.

Like in many other industries, there is ample opportunity to be successful however it remains a buyer beware industry. If you do not have competency and established relationships, there is much room for error. However, you increase your chances for success if you have, or partner with those who have, experience and a proven track record.

With that said, NO ONE can guarantee your personal success. Some factors affecting your success will be out of one's control such as market conditions, competition, certain borrower actions, and property values. Also, some factors are within one's control and include the note buyer's level of effort, willingness to learn, and treatment of relationships within the industry.

The content provided in this book is for informational purposes only. It should not be considered legal or financial advice. You should consult with an attorney or other professional to determine what may be best for your individual needs.

Neither Martin Saenz, 2nd Chance Funding, LLC nor Powerhouse Publishing make any guarantee or other promise as to any results that may be obtained from using the information in this book. No one should make any investment decision without first consulting his or her own financial advisor, attorney, CPA, etc. and conducting his or her own research and due diligence. To the maximum extent permitted by law, the author, publisher and 2nd Chance Funding, LLC disclaim any and all liability in the event any information, commentary, analysis, opinions, advice and/or recommendations prove to be inaccurate, incomplete or unreliable, or result in any investment or other losses.

INTRODUCTION

If the idea of note investing is new to you, you are not alone. The US mortgage note investing community is a small, tight-knit group of pioneers, solving the problems created by the housing bubble burst of the late 2000s and making huge investment returns in the process.

I believe anyone - with a little mentoring and encouragement - can be successful in mortgage note investing. This book isn't meant to be an all-inclusive instruction manual, but it will introduce you to the world of note investing and, hopefully, you'll see the great potential in it that I did when I "stumbled upon" this unique opportunity.

My winding path to entrepreneurship and 2nd Chance Funding started early - at the ripe old age of 5 I was selling cleaned-up rocks to my neighbors. I loved the independence that having money brings, so I got a job at 13 and worked some job or other all the way through high school.

After I graduated college with my undergraduate degree, I got a job as a mortgage officer, where I was the second highest producer. I loved making money and making deals but hated the corporate environment.

So I enrolled in the Drexel University MBA program. But instead of starting my own business, I ended up managing a call center for a large retailer. I hated every minute of every day. I ended up getting fired from that job after three years because of my inability, or unwillingness, to "play the game." While struggling through my short lived corporate career, I managed to earn my M.S. in Project Management from George Washington University. Subconsciously, I was going back into the safe and secure loving arms of the university system as a means of real world avoidance.

Getting fired ended up being my blessing in disguise. By then I was married to my brilliant and lovely wife, Ruth, and after we lost the call center income, we decided to start a museum exhibit and signage company. With our earnings we started buying rental properties in the Washington DC metro area, which is how I discovered mortgage note investing.

This is by no means a get rich quick scheme - working out mortgage notes is a process that requires diligence and patience. But it's simple enough for anyone who wants to potentially get returns of over 30% to learn and succeed in. And investors who don't want to personally do the dirty work of borrower outreach, connecting with vendors, learning nuances of state law, etc. can earn passive returns.

I'm thankful that mortgage note investing was brought to my attention. I've found the perfect outlet for my independent, entrepreneurial self. It's allowed my wife and I to raise a beautiful family with three children and one on the way. It's enabled Ruth to be a stay-at-home, home schooling mom. Serving God, building a future for my family - this is my "why." Nothing else matters to me beyond that.

CHAPTER 1

LEARNING HOW AND WHERE TO BUY DISTRESSED MORTGAGE NOTES

An investment in knowledge pays the best interest.

— *Benjamin Franklin*

What is the difference between a mortgage and a note?

Throughout this book I'll be talking about notes and mortgages. Even though they are related, they're not the same thing. It's important to understand the difference.

What do I mean by a mortgage note?

A note, in general, is short for "promissory note." In real estate, it's essentially an IOU in which a borrower promises to repay the loan amount under certain terms to a lender. Usually it's monthly payments of principal and interest over 30 years. It's signed in blue ink by the people who agree to pay the debt and is sent to the lender.

How is that different from a mortgage?

A mortgage is what ties that note to a property that someone is purchasing. It gives the lender the right to take the property if the borrower fails to keep up with payments under the terms of the note. The mortgage is signed by the owners of the property being mortgaged, usually the same as the signers of the note.

Both documents are signed simultaneously at settlement when you purchase a home or take out a second mortgage. Because the note is held by the lender, the lender is able to sell it to other interested parties. Banks often do this when the note becomes distressed because it's easier for them to sell the note than to foreclose on the property.

I should explain that a distressed note is essentially a mortgage note that is in default. Typically, this means that the note is more than 90 days past due, so the borrowers had some circumstance that they've gone through and for whatever reason are unable to pay.

This is where I come in. Investors like myself purchase those notes and then reach out to borrowers, hoping to get them reinstated and current on their payments. We make high returns when that happens.

What is the current state of the distressed mortgage note industry?

There are billions of dollars of distressed mortgage notes across the US. We find ourselves in that position because in the 2000s, a lot of mortgage companies were creating mortgage loans that they shouldn't have. They were giving borrowers more money than those borrowers could afford to repay. With creative financing, such as ARM loan transactions, people started falling behind on their mortgages as interest rates began to creep up. Couple that with the economic crisis of 2007-2008 when a lot of people lost their jobs, or had to settle for part time work, and the situation became hopeless for them.

What is an ARM?

ARM stands for Adjustable Rate Mortgage. It's a mortgage loan that has a fixed interest rate for a short period of time, often two years, and after that it flips to a variable interest rate that's tied to the market. Often that variable rate is higher than the original rate and, depending upon market conditions, it can continue to increase over time.

Here's how it becomes a problem for people. Let's say you get a home mortgage for $100,000 at a fixed rate of 4%. At that time you know you can afford those $500 per month payments and everything looks good. But at month 25, when the ARM rate kicks in, the interest rate could start creeping up, and that $500 payment over the course of time could rise to $800-$900. However, you probably haven't seen a matching increase in your income level to support that additional debt servicing.

When that began to happen in the 2007-2008 timeframe, as people fell behind on their mortgage payments, banks accumulated billions of dollars of these distressed mortgage notes on their balance sheets.

Many of the distressed notes I deal with originated from 2006 to 2008. Since that time, the banks have managed to work out modification terms with some borrowers, or decided to foreclose on the properties. However, many banks found that it's more beneficial to sell that distressed mortgage note and get it off the books than to go through a lengthy and costly foreclosure process with the borrower. That's why there are so many notes out there in the marketplace from 10 years ago. They just keep getting passed around.

As it stands, banks are generally not very effective at delving into a borrower's financial situation, working out new terms, and creating a plan that the borrower can afford. They're heavily regulated so they don't have much flexibility. So, either the distressed note debt sits on their books or they sell it off to an investor like myself.

Why are distressed notes attractive to investors?

The reason note investing is becoming a booming business is that investors can purchase the distressed notes at deep discounts. We buy them for pennies on the dollar. Folks like me have the expertise and the resources to connect with the borrowers, find out what their situation is, and help them come back to the table and start performing on their loan again. Once they're making payments again, the note then has higher value than my purchase price, sometimes even as much as what the bank originally valued it at.

What type of education does one need to buy mortgage notes?

Anybody can learn to do this successfully, with certain conditions. You have to be willing to put in the work, and you must have the capital resources up front to purchase these mortgage notes, as well as the capital resources in reserve to get the notes back up to speed. With that said, it is encouraged to consider formal education in the fundamentals of note investing to avoid costly learning curves. I now offer some online education courses at noteinvestingmadeeasier.com

You also have the option to be a passive investor. If you have the necessary capital but don't want to be involved with the day-to-day operations, you can choose to team up with an expert partner, where they go out and do all the heavy lifting and potentially provide a nice return on your investment. Either way you go, I recommend giving yourself the gift of a formal education in note investing.

What's the importance of having systems in place prior to moving forward on a note purchase?

I wouldn't be as successful in this business as I am without certain systems in place. I put a strong emphasis on working systematically. And you, as a potential new investor, need to have an action plan before you ever buy your first note. It's similar to putting together a business plan that lays out what your resources are in terms of money, time and energy; what your objectives are; and what types of returns you're looking for as an investor. You have to treat this like a business, or else you're setting yourself up for failure from day one.

Once you have the action plan in place, you'll need to design systems to make sure you're performing due diligence on these notes. The first system I recommend involves sourcing the mortgage notes. There are places where you can buy quality mortgage notes from credible sellers, and you need to have systems in place to find and connect with those types of sellers so you're starting off on a good foot.

Next is analyzing the financials of the notes and the borrowers, themselves. Whenever I receive a note opportunity, I perform three rounds of due diligence on it. I have to have a consistent, systematic way of doing this, because I'm reviewing dozens of mortgage notes at a time, and I need to look at each note from the same lens and judge which are the notes that I want to investigate for myself.

After collecting what we in the industry call a "mortgage tape," which is a pool of mortgage notes, I first delve into the fair market values of the properties, to get an idea for the potential value of the notes.

Then I look at credit reports and evaluate those to get a sense of the borrowers' behavior. It's essential for anyone interested in note investing to know how to read and analyze a credit report because it is such a significant reflection of how the borrower will or won't work with you as an investor.

Finally, I look at background checks that could reveal more about the borrower. The more you do this, the quicker you'll be able to form an opinion of the type of borrowers you're dealing with and how you should move forward on a note.

I should explain that with the mortgage tape comes some bad seeds mixed in with the good ones. If you perform due diligence correctly, then you should have a big picture view that will allow you to project return on investment (ROI) from that whole mortgage note package before ever buying a single note. The hours you spend in systematic research of these notes will save you a lot of time and money later on, because you'll know which notes are potential winners, and which ones are bad seeds.

My objective is to always make at least 30% ROI - and I often achieve that. This is why I strongly believe in having these systems in place. At the end of the day, it really is a numbers game.

What I find is some folks come into the industry and decide they want to get their feet wet by sampling just one mortgage note to see how that works out. But you really need about a year for a mortgage note to start performing or to come to some form resolution. If you're spending a whole year for one mortgage note, then you're not getting an accurate picture of what the industry could do for you. You should be buying multiple notes at a time. You will find some notes that just don't pan out as you expected, but you'll also have some home runs that will more than make up for the duds that you purchase.

What are the differences between buying first and second mortgage notes?

In the note investing realm you'll have the opportunity to choose from first and second mortgage note opportunities, and there are key differences in how you approach each type.

The main difference between them is that, on average, the first mortgage notes are more expensive, both in terms of purchase price and "work out" expenses to get the note performing in some way.

The purchase price for a first mortgage note is higher than that of a second mortgage, because basically you're paying for the privilege of having the best chance of getting repaid, since the first mortgage note takes priority over the second.

First mortgage note expenses

There are multiple types of work out expenses on a first mortgage to resolve before your investment can start earning for you, the most significant being insurance and back taxes.

I've found that for most notes, it's been two to four years since a mortgage payment has been made. So that means it's likely the borrowers also haven't kept up with their property taxes and their homeowner's insurance.

Assuming the homeowner's insurance has lapsed, as the note holder, you'll have to pay for force-placed insurance, which will cover the property if any kind of damage occurs to it, such as a tree falling on the house or some other natural disaster damage, until the borrower can reinstate their regular policy or some other arrangement is made. This kind of insurance is more expensive than regular policies, so you need to take that into consideration when projecting your expenses.

Regarding back taxes, you need to understand that a tax lien will be created on a property by the county after a certain period of time - it varies from county to county - and the tax lien holder will most likely foreclose on that property to collect payment. Because the tax lien supersedes even the first mortgage note, you may find the property foreclosed out from under you if those taxes aren't paid back, with interest, right away.

First mortgage note discounts

As of right now, in 2017, you can expect a discount of anywhere from the low 40s to 70 cents on the dollar. The level of discount is tied to the property value and the risk level associated with getting a good ROI. Generally, the lower the cost of the note, the higher the risk of getting a desirable increase.

Oftentimes your objective is an exit strategy of turning the property around and reselling it as bank-owned property. So, for example, if a property has a fair market value of $120,000, and it's in a good, residential neighborhood with low crime, decent schools, and not next to an industrial park, you'll have more confidence that you'll be able to sell it for $100,000 - $110,000 if you have to foreclose on the property.

But if a property is valued at $60,000, chances are there is some crime in the neighborhood and the schools are subpar. This puts you at more risk because that $60,000 property could take a significant drop to $25,000 in the blink of an eye. Let's say you bought that note for $20,000. When you add in $10,000 of back taxes, force-placed insurance costs and some legal fees, that's about $34,000 out of your pocket. If it then sells for $25,000 and you're paying a realtor's minimum commission of $3,000, plus settlement costs, you're going to lose about $15,000 in that transaction.

I'd also like to add that the financial situation of the borrower may or may not impact the discounted value of the note. You certainly want to consider their situation in deciding whether or not to work with them, as part of your due diligence. But you can't assume that a better chance of payment comes from borrowers with more stable incomes and higher property values. I've worked with medical doctors and lawyers that have had trouble making payments, but then I have people that work at Wal-Mart, or they work two jobs, and because it's important to them from a moral standpoint to pay off debt, they actually do better. You never know until you really get into it and start interacting with borrowers.

Second mortgage note pros and cons

When it comes down to it, I prefer the second mortgage market because I've done better from a return perspective. As far as discounts go, you can expect to pay about 20 to 50 cents on the dollar for a second mortgage note that is behind a current first mortgage. So not only are you buying it at a lower price point, you don't have to worry about the forced-placed insurance, back taxes, etc. because the first mortgage company's handling all that. Quite simply, second mortgage notes require less out of pocket money, and that's why so many note investors can get a better ROI with them.

Lower prices also mean you're able to accumulate more second mortgage notes in your portfolio, which spreads out your investment risk.

That's not to say there aren't drawbacks to second mortgage notes. Bottom line, you're behind a first mortgage in repayment priority, which is what makes second mortgages less expensive, but also riskier. Their value tends to be more related to borrower behavior and less on measurable data such as equity, fair market value of the property, what's owed on the property, etc. So your projections can be a bit more subjective.

A great way to gauge how well a second mortgage note will do is to look at the status of the first mortgage. If the borrowers are current on their first mortgage payments, that can indicate they are emotionally tied in some way to being in the home, which means they will be more motivated to work out a way to stay.

A second mortgage note illustration

One likely scenario is that a borrower took out a second mortgage, say, in 2006 when someone came knocking at the door offering them $60,000 of cheap money, and they took it. They made the payments for a few years while they were at a low, fixed interest rate, but then once the ARM kicked in and payments for the first mortgage got out of hand, they chose to stop paying on the second, altogether.

But now, it's 2017, and they're in a different, hopefully better, financial situation. Perhaps, at the time, they just couldn't afford what the banks were charging them when the variable rate hit 18%. So if you, as the note holder, approach them offering an

8% interest rate, and a lower principal balance, which then lowers their monthly payment, that can take a huge burden off of them and will motivate them to come back to the table.

Once you get their loan modified and they start making payments again, that note you bought at 25 cents on the dollar is now at its full value. Paid over 30 years at 8% interest, it's a pretty good investment.

There's a certain finesse, an art, to working with the second mortgage borrowers and getting them back in paying mode. It's worth learning. Your mindset should be to ask yourself how you can help the borrower out of this difficult situation.

Where do you find mortgage note opportunities?

Before I get into finding note sellers, I need to contrast the note investing community with the real estate investing community. They couldn't be more different. Whereas you could trip over 10 realtors while walking down the street of your city, and you can make real estate deals and offers all over town, the note investing community is small. It's a heavy relationships game, where note sellers actually vet the buyers and are cautious about whom they sell to, because their reputation is at stake. So before you ask yourself, "where do I find well priced discounted mortgage note opportunities," you need to focus on your branding. Some questions to ask are:

- How are my business cards designed and what content do they convey? Do they resemble business cards your banker has or do they read, "we buy houses". If your objective is to embrace the note investing industry, then start acting like the bank and have all your marketing collateral resemble that a bank.

- Do you have a website? Most peer investors I know look at websites of people they are about to transact with. Does your website appearance tie into how your marketing material looks? Does it signal to potential partners, vendors, and sellers that you are someone they need to get close to because you are transacting in the note space at a high level.

- What is your social media presence? The note industry is made up of people scattered throughout the US and beyond and we all connect through social media and conferences. How often do you post helpful articles and constructive comments?

- What is your story? You marketing material, website, social media presence, conferences attended will all tell your story and what you are focused on.

- How do I best fit into the note industry? I recommend subscribing to my YouTube channel Note Investing Made Easier as there are a ton of videos on this very subject.

When they take a risk on you and give you an opportunity to buy good, qualified, credible notes and then you don't follow through with the purchase, you probably are going to get cut off. That seller isn't going to allow you to buy from them again.

Just to give you an idea of the process and how serious this is, once you talk to a seller, you typically have only three to five days to perform due diligence. Then once you've made the transaction, you need to consummate the purchase sale agreement by wiring funds that day, or the next day at the latest. If there's any monkey business, the seller will move on and you're likely to also be blacklisted throughout the selling community, because everyone talks to everyone else in this industry.

There are many online mortgage note selling platforms you can find with a Google search, but the most popular is FCI out of California (fciexchange.com). The note industry considers that more like retail buying, because you're going to usually pay a higher premium per note. And you'll have to sort through a lot more to find the good ones. I have transacted with FCI and they run a very smooth operation. It's a really good operation! But when you start doing this business on a full-time level, when you really get to know the direct sellers and form relationships, they'll call you with "off the street" opportunities, as they call it, and you can get some really great deals.

In conclusion, branding yourself as a note professional, spending time building relationships through social media and conferences, transacting on deals in a professional and ethical manner will lead to increasing your brand recognition which will lead to further deal opportunities.

How much capital does one need to invest in notes?

That leads to me to giving you an idea of how much investment capital you'll need. For a first mortgage note, you should plan for a $30,000 purchase price per note, and as I mentioned before, you don't want to invest in one at a time, so multiply that by the number you buy at once.

In addition, investors should have $10,000 per note in reserve to bring all property taxes current immediately and to cover other "work out" costs—legal fees, etc.—that I talked about before. One caveat to that is the more seasoned you are, the lower your costs, because you'll be able to navigate the process faster, cut legal fees drastically, do a lot of the leg work yourself, and have more effective communication with the borrowers.

But a new investor should plan on those figures.

For a second mortgage note, an investor can get a group of a few mortgage notes for $30,000 and will need to have about $5,000 per note in reserve to perform the work out on those notes.

CHAPTER 2

MAKE YOUR MONEY WHEN YOU BUY

Spending money is much more difficult than making money.

—Jack Ma

Now that I've covered some of the basics of note investing, let's talk about "due diligence"—the steps you'll need to take to maximize your opportunity of finding notes that have a higher potential of becoming winners. It's this systematic approach that really allows you to make your money when you buy, as I'll explain.

What are the due diligence steps to take when evaluating a note opportunity?

For every note I'm interested in, I go through three rounds of due diligence (see Appendix A). The process normally begins with the note seller forwarding an Excel spreadsheet with data for the mortgage note tape opportunity. Sometimes I'm able to cherry pick the notes, but other times I'll have to take down the entire note tape.

I have predetermined parameters I use to eliminate notes when I'm able to cherry pick. For example, right off the bat I'll weed out certain states, bankruptcy statuses and property types. In cases where cherry picking is not allowed, I still have to know what the value of each of those notes is for myself, so I perform the three-round due diligence process even for notes that fall outside of my desired parameters.

First round goals

In the first round I start by reformatting the note seller's data into an Excel template I have created. I then plug the data from the tape into my template to really understand what I have as a whole. I'll be looking for information on fair market property values, mortgage data and borrower data.

First I search out fair market values of the property. This is just a preliminary look, using Zillow, Trulia, Realtor.com and some of the other property websites to look at prices, which I document in my spreadsheet. Typically, those values are inflated by about 10%, so for my general rule of thumb, I take the lowest value I find online and make that my gauge for fair market value.

Next I go into the collateral file to read the mortgage and understand how the note is structured. I check to make sure all the documents are in place, with proper chains of ownership. I'll go to the county website to get information on the back tax situation, because I'll have to pay any unpaid taxes due if I'm buying a first mortgage note. Most likely I'll also have to pay for force-placed insurance on that property if I'm buying the first mortgage. If it's a second mortgage note, I'll look to see if I can find any data on the status of first mortgage note.

Then I'll move on to looking for data about the borrowers themselves. I'll look at credit reports and skip tracing tools that let me compile a lot of information about people, such as past employment, tax assets, court records, business registration, etc. I delve down into the borrowers' situation as much as I can in a few minutes' time.

I try to run through things pretty quickly at this point because I could receive a note tape opportunity with 20 to 30 notes to evaluate in three to five days. I really want to find the notes that fit in my parameters and will work for me. So, in my first round of due diligence, I spend only about 30 minutes researching each note, projecting returns, and deciding if it will move on to the second round of evaluations.

Second round goals

The notes that meet my parameters go into my Round Two bucket. I'll pay for Broker Price Opinions (for first mortgage notes), or Automated Valuation Reports (for second mortgage notes). These reports will give me a more realistic understanding of the fair market value of the property. I document these updated values in my spreadsheet and use them as my primary value for each property.

These reports can range in cost from $20 to $100 and, in some cases, give you examples of comparable sold and listed properties. They include detailed descriptions and exterior photos of the property so you can better understand what you're looking at.

Next I'll go back to the real estate websites for deeper level research. Those sites are great for information on crime data statistics and for how the school systems are rated for that neighborhood. You also can go to rentometer.com and look at what the current rent is for a particular property. I make note of that data in my spreadsheet. All of that information gives me a feel for what the neighborhood is like and if there are any red flags.

For the mortgage due diligence, if I checked the county website in the first round, in round two I'll call the county treasurer as verification.

And finally, I'll do a more thorough review of the credit report to understand the borrowers' profiles and what their motivations are, as well as go through skip tracing data with a finer tooth comb. I'll do what's known as a PACER search to see the borrowers' bankruptcy status. This search also provides a wealth of information if the borrower has filed bankruptcy as they have to divulge a wealth of information about themselves personally and financially. If I have interest in that note, I'll go through that information in hopes of gaining a better insight into that borrower. Finally, any notes that pass my filters get moved into a third round of evaluations.

Third round goals

Before I do anything in round three, I review everything that I covered in rounds one and two to ensure I didn't miss anything. By that point, I'll start to have a good understanding of the property and the borrowers' situation. I might find that it's a vacant property or that the borrower is renting out the property and living somewhere else. I might look at a credit report and see someone's not paying their mortgage but they owe $30,000 to Nordstrom's and other high end stores, and they have a BMW financed for $40,000.

All this gives me a profile. Are the borrowers image driven or are they frugal? Do they have the income that they would need to pay on the note? Sometimes the credit reports will list places of employment so you can get a feel for their household income. These are the things that map out who the borrower is. Regarding the overall value of the property is, I ask myself, "Is the property in a good location, with good schools, or not? Is it a blighted property?"

This is where being truly diligent really pays off, because I'd say probably 8 out of 10 times I miss something in round one or round two that I catch in round three, which can materially change my perspective of that note, the borrower and the property.

After this extra careful round of the due diligence process, I'm able to project what I'm willing to pay for that note, which is why I say I make my money when I buy. Once you've been doing this awhile, you'll have a better feel for what your work out costs will be. But for beginners, a good rule of thumb is $5,500 for legal fees to work out a first mortgage and $4,000 for second mortgage notes. There are other costs which may accrue as well, such as unpaid property taxes on first mortgage notes. More on that later.

So now that I have a good idea how much it's going to cost to work out the exit strategy and what my projected return is, and I'll know if I want to seek a deed in lieu from the borrower and help them move on from their situation.

What is a deed in lieu?

A deed in lieu is when the borrower signs over the property to the mortgage note holder. Typically, when they do that, the note investor will release the borrower from any liability on that property and obligation on any debt owed. This is common with borrowers who have been involved in divorce. People just want to move on and they don't want to have this heavy debt looming over their heads while living in a house that's associated with such negative memories.

Whether it's a deed in lieu, where the borrower is getting out from under the debt, or they're signing a loan modification for more favorable payment terms to get them back on track with paying, I'm able to project a sound exit strategy from each note and combine those numbers into an overall projected ROI from that entire note tape opportunity.

What are popular exit strategies when buying notes?

Besides deed in lieu and loan modification strategies, there are other options, such as obtaining the property outright to rent out, or an early discounted payoff. However, it's important to know there are so many unexpected turns that the mortgage note can take once you begin to work it out that you won't know what your actual exit strategy is for a given property will be until the end of the process.

For example, you might buy a note with the borrowers living in the house, but then when you press them for resolution, they may decide to move out and fall off the grid. Then you have to adjust and move to another exit strategy. The bottom line is that knowing all the exit strategies that are available to you from the start will help you transform that note into a profitable status.

The Golden Rule for note investing - the ideal scenario - is to do a loan modification that helps the borrower get back on their feet. Then you'll have a note that's bringing in cash flow every month, and you'll also have an asset you can sell, or resell on the note marketplace for a much higher premium.

If you can't achieve that, you'll want to work on getting the property back in shape quickly so you can rent it out, resell it, etc.

Another popular exit strategy is the early discounted payoff, which is where the borrower gives you a lump sum amount at a discount. This early payoff can mean bigger yields for you, in the long run.

Depending on the situation, there are times I choose to sell notes that I've gotten performing again or to keep notes that are performing well and providing long term returns.

How does one combine due diligence and exit strategies to formulate a projected ROI from a note purchase?

Even if I have 20 notes that I'm looking at as a group, I view each individual note as a separate asset. After I have completed all three rounds of due diligence, looked at the estimated work out costs and potential returns on my spreadsheet, I come up with a figure I'm willing to pay for each note, then I combine those projections into one offer. I go back to the seller and see if we can come to an agreement.

Once I've bought the notes, I give myself 12 months before the notes work out, so month 13 is the start of the true first year. That's going to be the most profitable one, because by then I'll potentially have notes with loan modifications that are bringing in monthly payments, plus any deeds in lieu can be resold for a return at that point. From year two to year thirty my ROI on that tape portfolio will drop off. So my focus in projections is really that true first year. That's how I'll determine the value I'll be willing to pay for the tape. At this point it's just a matter of whether the note seller will accept my offer.

Ready to make an offer? What now?

Depending on the relationship I have with the seller, I'll approach making my offer in different ways. Over time you'll get to know these sellers. If you have some key relationships in place, you can send an email, maybe a one page letter of intent, to the seller and just say, "I'm looking at these six notes and this is what I'm willing to pay." The note seller always has a Note

Sale Agreement template ready to go if they choose to accept your offer.

If they don't have any other offers on the table, and your offer is within the range of what they're looking to fetch, then they'll consummate the deal right away. If they're waiting on offers from other potential investors to come in, they may tell you they're holding off for those. The seller's objective is to sell their entire note opportunity. However, if they don't see much interest in that note tape, then you might find they're willing to let you pick out and buy the notes you want.

The key to making a good offer is having credibility as a buyer. These sellers know that if I make an offer, I'm going to wire money that day or the next, and I'm ready to roll. Plus, my offers are respectable. I'm not going to try to low ball the seller, and they know this, so they're more likely to work with my offer. Again, if you have built a brand and established yourself as someone who is a player in the note space, you transact on deals with honor, you will be received favorably from the sellers. In a sense, in the note space, people sell to people they like and trust on a peer to peer level.

But if you're just starting out and don't have a track record for sellers to look at, I would recommend emailing a formal letter of intent, along with proof of funds. That will go a long way with sellers. Your letter of intent needs to include descriptive language with a plan of action for buying the notes, letting the seller know you understand how the process works, that you're serious and that you'll be ready to wire the money right away.

I'd just like to re-emphasize here that, in the mortgage note industry, you need to do what you say you're going to do. In the real estate industry you can hop from city to city and you can put out 100 offers at a time with 100 different realtors and make money doing that. But the note industry is a very tight-knit group. Everyone comes together at conferences. Everybody comes together on Facebook, and through a variety of other forums. So if you show that you're a credible investor, you're going to be welcomed into the community. It's a very positive experience to be welcomed in, and those relationships can spell profits for you.

Appendix A: Three Rounds of Due Diligence

	Task
Round 1	Receive Seller's Excel spreadsheet note tape and reformat it using in-house template
	Assuming you can cherry pick off the tape, remove notes that fall far outside your predetermined parameters (i.e. States you're avoiding, BK statuses, property types, etc). If there is no cherry picking allowed, look over the tape and determine if you can work with the notes given your parameters. This is a high level look over.
	Google search each property address and go through each online real estate website (i.e. Zillow, Realtor.com, Trulia, etc.) Document each value in your spreadsheet and use the lowest value as your assumed preliminary Fair Market Value.
	On notes you are interested in, go to county websites and look up property taxes to determine if there are any back taxes owed
	Analyze the credit report and any borrower communication located in the file
	Given the data provided by the seller, the assumed FMV, the back tax situation, and the credit report, determine which notes you which to pursue or if you wish to move forward with the tape in general.

Round 2	With your reduced list, order Broker Price Opinion reports for 1st mortgage notes and Automated Valuation Reports for 2nd Mortgages. This will give you a more realistic idea of the true FMV and allow you to compare notes with the internet website site values. Document these FMV's in the spreadsheet and use them as your primary value for the property.
	Go back to the internet real estate sites like Zillow and Trulia to determine crime in the area, local school ratings, and property value trends for that area. Go to Rentometer.com and determine rental values. Note your finds in your spreadsheet.
	Do a PACER search on any bankruptcies for the borrower(s). There are certain cases where note buyers seek out notes with bankruptcies, but if you are just starting out, be careful with these. There is an entirely separate expertise in buying bankruptcy related notes. Document your findings in the spreadsheet in terms of BK filing, type, resolution, etc.
	Re-read through the credit report and determine a borrower profile picture. Document your findings in a comment section of the spreadsheet. This step is extremely important as you can grab your odds of getting a loan modification from the credit report in many cases.
	Further weed out notes based on your findings. Here will be a point when you will finally begin to understand which notes are great, fair, and poor.

Round 3	The notes you wish to purchase determine a price per note you are willing to pay factoring in current market pricing. Low balling the seller is not a good strategy in the note industry so be fair with your offering. If you have a note that is great or fair, your margins are built into the buy from the onset.
	For each note, determine how much workout expenses each will take. This will come with some experience but do your best if you are starting out. A rule of thumb is $5,500 for legal fees to work out a 1st mortgage and $4,000 for the 2nd's.
	Determine the exit strategy and returns per each note.
	Roll up your numbers for an overall analysis of the note purchase and place an offer based on thorough due diligence.

CHAPTER 3

NOTE INVESTING IS A TEAM SPORT

The richest people in the world look for and build
networks; everyone else looks for work.

— *Robert Kiyosaki*

Mortgage note investing isn't a cut-and-dried, number crunching type of business that you can do anonymously behind a computer screen. It requires building relationships based on trust and cooperation. If you truly want to succeed, it's incredibly important to form a network of people in various industries, including other note investors, loan servicers, lawyers and other vendors.

How important are peer relationships?

The main reasons to have a peer network are so you can get information and education on an ongoing basis and to learn from others' experiences. After you've established some good relationships, you can use your peer network to form partnerships and pool resources to go after larger purchases.

As I've mentioned before, the note investment industry is a very tight-knit group. It's a warm group, with people who are willing to help. But you also have to show you're willing to learn and be ready to reciprocate and help others when they need it.

Sometimes you'll need guidance with legal or tax matters. Sometimes you'll need moral support. There's wear and tear to this industry and if you're in the middle of a grueling legal process, trying to connect with the borrowers and bring them to the table, it helps to have someone to bounce ideas off of or to explain the situation to. Those relationships help you get through the note process.

Not only have I found really strong peer relationships, I've also found good friendships. There are two women that I've linked up with, Cathy Cray and Cathie Jeffs with PAC - Paper Assets Capital - in New Jersey. They've formed a successful mastermind group called Women In Notes or WIN. We've become friends and I wanted to support their efforts, so I've co-launched a DC regional event for WIN. We're working together to grow the educational piece to this industry.

Making connections

The best way to start connecting with other investors is by going to note conferences, which are held across the country. And you can also connect with other note investors on social media, such as Twitter and Facebook.

One well-known conference is the Paper Source Note Symposium in Las Vegas. There are also a lot of regional ones that are held by Real Estate Investment Clubs. The best way find them is through a Google search.

When you find some groups you're interested in joining, the most important thing is just to be up front and honest and tell them exactly where you're at. If you're a newbie and you've read a few books and you're just looking to test out the waters with mortgage notes, then say that. We all understand that everyone has to start someplace.

There are many people who have helped me grow in my journey as a note investor. They are fellow note investors I've done business transactions with, but more than that, they're people I rely on for guidance. A few of these are Deepta Hiremath, with Allied Note Investors; Bill McCafferty, with Peoples Debt Relief Solutions; and Frank Buono, with B&B Capital Management.

Occasionally you may find yourself in a jam and can't figure out a solution on your own. I once had to take back a property that was a second mortgage. When you take back a second mortgage property, you take it back contingent upon the first mortgage, so here I had this property and didn't know what to do with it. I connected with some of my peers, and they gave me guidance on how to rent out the property subject to the first. The property was in Michigan, a good distance away from where I'm at. But with guidance I was able to set up a tenant in the location and rent out the property with success.

How do you find the right loan servicer?

The next type of relationship that I want to talk about is with your loan servicer. I'll start off by explaining what a loan servicer is and what they do for you.

If you have a mortgage on your home, most likely you receive monthly statements from the lender or the servicer telling you when and where to remit payment, the current balance, last payment received, break out of principle and interest, etc. At the end of the year, they'll send you the tax forms for you to submit to your CPA. As a note investor, I outsource these functions to the loan servicer. They also keep up with the numerous regulations and compliance issues, so it's critically important to have that note set up through a loan servicer when the loan modification is put in place.

There are many loan servicing companies to choose from, and some of the most popular are FCI Lender Services, Land Home Financial Services and Madison Management Service.

Selecting a loan servicer

My priority in choosing a loan servicing company is speed in responsiveness. How long is it taking the loan servicer to process payments? Are they mailing out the monthly statements on time? Are they reporting on the borrower's credit report? What's the schedule for getting my payment after the borrowers make their payments? There are some loan servicers that will pay you within a week of receiving payment, but with other loan servicers you have to wait 30 to 45 days to receive your money. That has a huge impact on your cash flow.

If you're new to the industry, or you want to be a hands-off kind of investor, you can have the loan servicer do a full collection effort for you. They can do all the skip tracing, borrower outreach, handle the legal portion of thing - everything an active note investor does - for a monthly fee.

Or you can be a little more hands-on and use the lender's non-collection, non-loss mitigation service, where they're just sending the monthly statements for you. That allows you as the note investor to piggyback off of those statements when you're reaching out to the borrowers. This is important because if the borrowers haven't been getting monthly statements for a long time and then suddenly start getting them again, that gets their attention. It lets them know you're serious. But it's also a tool that helps you reach out to them and tell them you're there to help them get back on track and not to punish them.

The monthly statements are an important service and worth paying for. I would like to emphasize that, if you are going to do your own borrower outreach, you need to understand collection laws in each state and have a firm grasp on the Federal Fair Debt Collection Act.

Each servicer will have a representative that you can interact with. When the loan is in a non-performing state, there will have to be more dialogue with that representative, so it's important that they're responsive and can help you through any situations you're having. When you get a loan modification in place, they have to be able to process it, make adjustments on their end and do everything possible to make a smooth transition for the borrower who's looking to start paying again. You want to have a good working relationship with that person.

If you're new, it may seem intimidating to work with a loan servicer, but if you contact any of the ones I mentioned, I know they'll be welcoming. They'll send you a service agreement wherein you'll commit that note to them for a certain period of time, and they'll outline what services they're going to provide to you to service the note and at what cost. They have no problem working with someone new. But they're not there to educate you, so you should plan to get the information you need about the note investing process from the people you meet at the mastermind groups, conferences, social media networks, etc.

Investors should understand that the loan servicer can only be as successful as the quality of the note. So if you purchased a good note with good potential, and you're able to come to terms with a borrower, then a servicer will be able to help that come to fruition. However, if you bought a bad note—no servicer, no peer network, no legal team is going to be able to resuscitate that investment.

How do you build the right seller relationships?

As I mentioned earlier, it's important to have a good relationship with note sellers, built on trust, so you can find out about good opportunities and have a better chance of your offers being accepted. New investors will most likely begin by using online platforms, like I've mentioned. FCI has an online exchange, and loanmls.com is another popular loan exchange site. You can log in and sift through notes and make purchases. It's pretty streamlined and easy to do. As long as you have the money, you can buy notes.

As you get more experienced, you can initiate relationships with note sellers at conferences and in mastermind groups.

Sometimes getting a good opportunity comes down to having friends in the business. Just today I wired money to buy two performing notes from a friend who owned them and wanted to liquidate and recapitalize quickly, so she gave me a call. I'd like to reemphasize that's it's so important to do what you say you're going to do, conduct yourself with honor, and always be out there helping other peers and learning as much as you can. That approach opens a door to ongoing deal flow.

The connections I've been able to make have been amazing just from being active in some Facebook investing groups. When I go to conferences, I run into sellers that I've had minor exchanges with, or that recognized me from some of my social media posts, and we have an instant connection. They wouldn't have known me from Adam otherwise, and we wouldn't have had an opportunity to connect at a deeper level.

Another way to ensure a good relationship with sellers is, after you go through the due diligence process and determine an offer price, make sure it is a fair offer. Low balling is highly frowned upon in this industry, and you could get blacklisted. When you see a portfolio of notes that's viable, despite price increases over the past few years, there are still high profit margins to be had. As I've said before, sellers are conscious of maintaining a good reputation.

So put in a fair offer and when that offer has been accepted, wire the funds immediately. Don't try to stretch out the process. Also, don't try to change terms after you've agreed upon a price and terms with the seller. All of that leads to very bad feelings and you're going to have a harder time finding a seller who will work with you. This industry self-regulates in that way.

People will pick up on whether or not you're a straightforward, consistent person, even if they've never met you in person. For me, it's a priority to treat people honorably and to maintain integrity. I've got a family to feed that I love very much, and this is the passion that drives my business, so I don't want to do anything to jeopardize that. I try to give it all I have.

How do you build the right legal team?

A note investor should have a good creditor rights attorney in every state. There are some law firms that stretch out over various states, but you should have the whole US map covered. One of the best ways to start finding attorneys is through your peer network. Find out who's using what attorneys and see if you can find some winners, as well as the "do not ever use" list as well. It's always out there.

I like to work with law firms that offer a la carte pricing, which means they have a set price for each service they perform and don't require you to pay a retainer up front. For example, when they send out a demand letter to a borrower, you know that service is going to cost you X amount. When they file a complaint against a borrower, you know they'll always charge you Y amount. Or the title pull is Z amount. There's a specific price for every step of the process, so you can decide what you need them to do, and what you can do yourself. As long as that borrower isn't contesting the foreclosure motion in any way, you'll be able to have a pretty clear estimate of what your legal expenses will be.

But there are other law firms that will say, "Sign the retention letter and send us a check for $5000 (for example) to start work." If you send them that check, you can be sure that they're going to spend every penny of it. You've lost control of the spending process at that point, which is something I don't care to do.

Once you've decided to work with a given law firm or attorney, make sure you pay them on time. There are note investors that stretch out payments because they're riding out money, or their cash flow is tight, or they're trying to preserve investor capital. But if that attorney's performing a good service for you, you need to pay them on time. They will respect that. They're going to answer your call before they answer other calls, and they'll be more prompt with servicing your account.

These attorneys are sophisticated, and they go after people who owe money for a living! Don't be one of those people that they go after! They'll cut you off, and that's not good for your reputation. Keep in mind that these creditor rights attorneys don't just work with you. They work with all your peers. They show up at the note investing events, too. So you want them to be saying nice things about you, which ties together with building those peer relationships.

How do you build the right vendor relationships?

Outside of loan servicers and attorneys, which we already discussed, there are other third party vendors you need to partner with. You'll need to use door knockers—people who physically go to the door of the property and establish communication with the borrowers; information services like Credco and LexisNexis that you can pull credit information from; and skip tracing services, like TLO.

What is skip tracing?

I've mentioned skip tracing before, but this is a good place to explain it. Skip tracing is the industry name for the process of doing background checks on borrowers. If borrowers have a legal obligation to you, you're allowed to perform skip tracing on those individuals, so you can get information on where they work, any kind of criminal activity that they've been involved in, where their primary residence is, current emails or phone numbers, etc. It just gives you insight into that borrower's world so you can have better outreach success later on. It's helpful to partner with skip tracing services to help you move the process along faster.

Relationships with construction trades companies

In cases where your intent is to resell or rent out the property, there are companies like US Best Repair Service, where you can order essentially any type of REO (Real Estate Owned property) service, anywhere in the country. They'll do anything from changing locks, fixing windows, touching up paint, lawn maintenance, whatever is needed to get that property up to where it needs to be in order to resell it. You can access them through their website, email or phone calls.

That's the beauty of the note investing industry. You can do note investing from anywhere in the country even though you almost never go see the properties firsthand. And that's why it's so important to have a solid relationship with your vendors. You'll be relying heavily on those local vendors who are your eyes when you're not there.

What is credit pulling?

When you become a note investor, you will want to sign up with a service whereby you can pull borrower's credit reports. The information from the credit reports provides valuable information such as identifying information, trade lines, credit inquiries, and public record information. The data the borrower has on their report and doesn't have on their report tells a clear story about the borrower. You'll need to spend ample time reading each report and visualizing the borrower's story. Your success in this industry depends on it.

What is title pulling?

For title pulling services I recommend ProTitleUSA when pulling Full Title Search reports and Ownership & Encumbrance (O&E) reports. Normally, for the note industry, I'm pulling the O&E report which gives me information on all the liens, mortgages, judgements, tax status on the property, and a copy of the vesting deed. This gives a clear story on the ownership of the property along with any claims against the property.

What is the difference between a Broker Price Opinion (BPO) and a Automated Valuation Report (AVM)?

Whenever I buy a 1st mortgage note, I pull a BPO report and whenever I buy a 2nd mortgage note, I pull an AVM report.

The BPO report is provided by a real estate agent that goes to the physical property and takes exterior pictures. They then provide a report giving exterior pictures, property pricing, real property comparisons, and market evaluation. The AVM report is computer generated through mathematical modelling and provides property pricing given real property comparisons.

What are some key success factors in maintaining these relationships?

The best advice I can give about fostering and maintaining good relationships with your vendors is that you should spend ample time getting prepared to give them what they need so they can do the best job for you. Let's say you're setting up door knocking services with a vendor like NCCI. They go out and knock on doors for the note investors so they can connect with the borrowers. The more information you can give them up front about the borrowers and the details of your note, the more effective job they're going to do when they're standing face-to-face with the borrowers.

Or say you're setting up services for a Notice of Default letter to go out from a law firm. If you give them all the assignments, all the note and mortgage documents, then not only can they send out the letters, they can also have a better understanding of the collateral file situation. They'll be able to give you recommendations for things you may not have thought of that need to be adjusted, or how to navigate the complaints stage of the foreclosure process.

The more prepared you are in what you give to your vendors, the more success the vendors are going to have, and the less money it's going to cost you. I may not need to send the door knockers out as much if I'm giving them more information up front. I may not need to go as long and as far into the foreclosure process if I'm giving the lawyers all the information they need up front. Do your homework, get the vendors what they need to make good decisions, and it will benefit you financially and emotionally.

CHAPTER 4

TURNING A NON-PERFORMING NOTE INTO A PERFORMING NOTE

Opportunity is missed by most people because it is dressed in overalls and looks like work.

— *Thomas Edison*

In this chapter we'll look more specifically at the effort, from meticulous document management to borrower outreach, that goes into transforming a non-performing note, on which the borrower is behind or has stopped making payments, into one that will create a positive return. The first step is getting familiar with the contents of the collateral file.

How to ensure your collateral file is in order

The collateral file is the collection of records from the note seller, which I'm now responsible for maintaining as the note owner. It contains:

- The original mortgage
- The original note
- The original allonge
- Assignment of mortgage
- Credit reports

- Prior correspondence with the borrowers
- Skip trace documents (if applicable)
- Loan modification agreements between the borrowers and a prior lender (if applicable)

Allonges

An allonge is a permanent addendum to the original note that shows there's been an endorsement - an ownership transfer to the note buyer - that there wasn't room for on the original note. This is important for showing chain of ownership of the note.

Assignments of Mortgage

The assignment of mortgage is essential, as well. It's the document that indicates that there's been a legal transfer of that mortgage, along with all the rights and duties, to a new lender. The lender takes that assignment of mortgage and gets it recorded at the county recorder's office where the property is located.

Receiving the collateral file

The collateral files comes as electronic documents when you're performing due diligence prior to the note purchase. However, when you consummate the note's sale agreement, having wired the funds to make the purchase, you'll receive the physical collateral file document in the mail. Normally, you should receive that file within a few weeks.

That's another aspect of due diligence I didn't mention earlier. Before making an agreement, you want to make sure the note seller is in possession of the physical file and find out how long it will take you to receive it once you've made a purchase.

Missing items in the collateral file

There could be missing signatures on the note or mortgage that would hinder your legal claim to that asset - the mortgage note - if it had to go through foreclosure. There also could be missing links in the chains of allonges and assignments of mortgage. For example, if the mortgage had been sold by the original lender to a hedge fund, which sold it to an investment capital firm, which turned around and sold it to a private investor, who sold it to you, then you're fifth in line in that chain. You want to make sure the correct allonges and assignments were completed and recorded for each step of the process, otherwise that also may hinder your legal claim.

Examining the collateral file can be a bit tedious, but it's critical to the successful transformation of the note. If you discover problems they are usually fixable, but it does require the discipline to go line by line.

You'll also need to have an understanding of individual state laws across the country. There are some states where, if you are missing a link in the chain, you could be prevented from fulfilling foreclosure claim against that borrower. It could create all kinds of legal chaos because of stalling from the borrower's side.

There are other states that allow you to file an affidavit for the missing allonge or assignment of mortgage. Once you get those recorded, it firms up the chain.

Keep in mind that you'll be looking at potentially dozens of notes at one time, so don't rely on memory. It's important to have a system by which you organize that collateral file when you receive it so you can spot when there's a problem. I have a digital filing system that's universal for all my notes. I sort all the documents based on that filing system, and I house that on an online shared drive that I always have access to, wherever I am.

How to conduct borrower outreach

Once you have the note and mortgage details squared away, the next step is to open lines of communication with the borrowers. Some borrowers probably aren't going to be as excited to hear from you as they should be, because they may have been threatened in the past by other lenders, and they have no idea who you are. You'll want to use every tool at your disposal to contact and inform them of your role and how to move forward.

I keep a folder of numerous forms that I use to connect with the borrower. You will find forms are living documents and you will update and make enhances over the course of time. Some I have spent a good deal of legal cost and time crafting. Either way, it is good to have a library in place so you can become more efficient when working with the borrower versus playing catch up in your outreach. Visit noteinvestingmadeeasier.com to learn more about what a good resource can do for you.

I send them a welcome package to get things rolling. It'll include a copy of the original mortgage and note and the assignment of mortgage showing the ownership's been transferred to me. I let them know about the loan servicer I've put in place so they know to expect to hear from them. The loan servicer will send them a RESPA "hello" letter, themselves.

RESPA stands for Real Estate Settlement Procedures Act. It's a federal regulation. Anytime there's a transfer of note ownership, the new note owner needs to send certain disclosures to the borrower. This establishes that the transfer's taken place and gives any details about how the borrower can contact the new owner of that note, or the new loan servicer that's managing the mortgage payments.

When I make that first contact my goal is to introduce myself and give the borrowers confidence that I'm not scamming them, that I actually do own that mortgage note and that they do now owe that money to me. However, my attitude is to be supportive and find out how their situation is at the time, and how I can work with them to help them get back on track. That's the Golden Rule of note investing, as I mentioned before. I can't best serve the borrower if I don't understand where they are, financially and emotionally.

In the initial welcome letter I extend the opportunity to have a discussion. There are times when the borrower will call me based on that first initial package. It's rare, maybe a 10% chance. When that happens, I may give them some options on where we could go from there. But I don't want to bog them down with too many options and confuse them at that initial point.

When to bring legal on

In most cases I'm buying notes where there are two to four years of default, so I'll bring in legal right away. I do it that way because it further legitimizes my claim to that mortgage note and lets the borrower know that, "I'm here. I'm for real. And I'm not going anywhere. It's in your best interest to talk to me sooner than later, because if we're talking later, it's going to be much more expensive for all of us."

Once I get the law firm involved, the documents they use are pretty cut and dried. They start with a Notice of Default letter, which states that the borrower's in default, shows the reinstatement fee, and lets them know they have 30 days (in most states) to restore what is owed to reinstate the loan, otherwise, further legal action may occur. It also shows the note owner's name and phone number to contact if they have any questions.

There are some states, like North Carolina, where you have to have certain licenses to make any direct connection with the borrowers. In those cases my attorney talks to the borrowers, as well as the licensed loan servicing company that's registered with those states.

How to piggyback off of legal and loan servicers to bring the borrower to the table

Just like getting legal involved can help prod the borrowers to speak with you, the actions taken by loan servicers can also help get across to the borrowers that you're now the lender they need to work with. There are two schools of thought on when to bring on loan servicers. Some investors wait for the loan to be modified or for some payments to start coming in before they set things up with the loan servicer. I tend to err on the side of caution and set up with the loan servicer immediately.

The loan servicer I use most often reports on the borrowers' credit report, so that's one tool I use up front to impact the borrowers' decision. I show them that their delay can hurt their credit report, which could be a nuisance if they're trying to finance a new car, or get a credit card. So that's one helpful "touch" the loan servicer provides. The other is the payment statements they send out every month. I look at them as the third arm for the outreach effort, after legal and myself.

Every time borrowers get a statement or serious-sounding document in the mail it "touches" their consciousness. You sent them a touch with the welcome packet, the lawyers sent them a touch or two, and then they're getting them from the loan servicers, as well. You'll want to leverage these touches to persuade the borrower to come back to the table. That's what I mean by "piggybacking" off of legal and loan servicers.

At this point in the process, getting borrowers to take action is really more of an art. Obviously you have regular systems in place - you're going to set up the file with the loan servicer and you're going to give legal all the documents they need to begin the foreclosure process with the Notice of Default letter. However, actually getting the borrower to the table is where the artistry comes in, and it boils down to understanding the borrowers' situation. Each one is different.

Strategies to engage with the borrowers

Let's say they're spend-aholics who aren't paying on a second mortgage note, which you now own. You can see from all the data you've compiled that they're spending money, and they're paying their first mortgage. So that tells you they have income coming from somewhere. In that case I would get in touch with them and see about getting them a payment plan that they can afford and get them back in the habit of paying on it every month.

Another situation could be with a first mortgage on a property that's worth $60,000 and they're two years behind on taxes, so right away I start paying those back taxes to get things current. But I can see the borrowers are being dodgy and avoiding everybody on their credit report. In this case I'll be a bit more aggressive with the door knocking, or with fast-tracking the foreclosure process, which kind of twists someone's arm to come to the table.

Or let's say the borrowers can't afford to live where they're living, so they've been paying other bills just to get by, but not the mortgage. I see a lot of people in that situation. I would probably recommend they do a deed in lieu and sign over the property to me. I relieve them of any further obligation with that mortgage. Then I can resell the property, rent it out, etc.

Despite all the work I put it to establish a relationship with them, I would say I never hear from around 30% of the borrowers, even throughout the foreclosure process. That could be for a variety of reasons. Maybe they're mentally exhausted, or they're just trying to live for free for as long as they can, or they've decided to walk away from the situation. But 70% of the time I'll hear from them in some way, whether it's when they file bankruptcy and I get notified by their attorney, or when they hire an attorney to go through the loan modification process, or some other exit strategy, with me. Or sometimes they'll just call me on the phone.

What's sad to me is I see a lot of people that will get a lawyer because they've been convinced by the lawyer that he or she will get them the best deal and make sure they're not being taken advantage of. But then the borrower has to pay that lawyer, plus they're still going to have to pay me, so their costs have just gone up.

In reality the borrowers get the most favorable deal by talking to me as soon as possible. The longer they wait, or their lawyers delay the process, the more my costs accrue, and that gets passed on to them.

How to firm up an agreement once you have a connection with the borrower

Once you succeed in getting borrowers to the table, there are a variety of options you'll have as the lender to seal the deal and get them to put pen to paper. It really depends on what exactly both the borrower and I are trying to achieve. That will determine the course of action. If they want to get caught up and back on track right away, we'll create a loan modification document, get it blessed by legal, and consummate it with the borrower. That's the ideal scenario, of course.

There are also other exit strategies, like early discounted payoff, where they just want to pay one lump sum and have this problem go away. Other times, they want to use their county or state mediation program, if available.

One thing you may run into that could slow your progress is there are some bankruptcy attorneys and debtors' rights attorneys who maximize their fees by dragging things out or by encouraging the borrowers to file bankruptcy. The borrowers think they can do something and then they figure out later they can't do it, so they hesitate to move forward. But for those who decide to work with me directly, I can tell you, we'll figure something out that's good for both of us, and do so very quickly.

What do you do after the agreement is in place?

Once the borrowers have agreed and signed to the new terms, you submit that loan modification or other agreement to the loan servicing company, because the payments have to go through them to keep everything in one place, and to keep everything legal. Sometimes the arrears payments get sent to the loan servicer, too, depending on the arrangement you have. But ultimately, the borrowers should make monthly payments directly to the loan servicer. All of this information will be included in the collateral file for the mortgage.

After you get the loan modification in place and everything's set up and working, it's important that you keep in good communication with the borrowers. I check in with them every few months to see how things are going. I also stay on top of the loan servicer's activities by checking their website dashboard to view when payments are coming in, or to find out if there's been any email or phone correspondence with the borrowers and what was discussed.

I work to get the borrower set up on an auto-pay, so the money's taken directly out of their account every month. That also helps keep things on track. You're kind of in babysitting mode, if you will, for the first year. But once you get through that first year of seasoning, there's a significantly higher potential for that loan to keep performing until the borrower pays it off, sells the house, or what have you.

What is the value of a note after it is performing?

Over a period of time the note increases in attractiveness once the borrowers are consistently making their payments on time, you've covered all the arrears, and gotten things back on the right track. This is what I mean by seasoning the note. This can have a huge impact on the note's value, as well as on communities as a whole.

I like to look at this process with a macro view. You have a positive impact on the borrowers, who are relieved to be back in compliance with a more affordable payment. Now they don't feel like they have to be on the run from creditors. So you've just changed their lives for the better. That, in turn, helps bring stability to the neighborhood, because you have more people in the community who can afford to live there and feel more invested in it. Stable communities help our country as a whole be healthier.

When I've done everything I can to get an affordable loan modification for the borrowers, they truly appreciate what I've done. They've moved from an emotional state of being terrified and losing sleep to one where they can breathe again and feel good about the fact they're meeting their obligations and can keep their family in the house. From a note investor standpoint, that relationship is priceless. It means that when they have a choice, they're going to make a more conscious effort to make payments to me versus the payments to a credit card company, or some other cost that they've been diverting money to over the years. That's when all my work pays off and it's really special.

One of the reasons I love this industry is that there are a lot of us in the note investing community that feel this way. Anytime I meet with my peers at events and conventions, we talk about it. It is just a numbers and cents game to the banker that originated the mortgage loan, or hedge fund manager that bought $100 million of these loans at huge discounts. But private note investors are just as passionate about helping borrowers as they are making good profits.

CHAPTER 5

INVESTMENT OPTIONS FOR THE AVERAGE PERSON

We make a living by what we get, but we make a life by what we give.

— *Winston Churchill*

The goal of this chapter is to give you a vision of how you too can generate income through investing in mortgage notes, even if you've never invested in real estate before. I've had a successful note investing business for several years, and through the guidance and encouragement I've received from mentors and peers, as well as the personal interactions I've had with borrowers, I've grown both as a business owner and as a person.

I believe this business can benefit you financially while empowering you to have a positive impact on others, which can affect entire communities, as I'll explain. And since you're probably interested in establishing a note investing business sooner rather than later, in this chapter I'll tell how you can get started with investments right away.

What type of success have you had in the note business?

My involvement in note investing has been fantastic. It has transformed my life. I've been able to build a portfolio of cash-flowing assets which pays money every month into my LLC. Another portfolio of performing notes provides cash flow into my IRA, as well as my wife's IRA.

In other cases I have gotten a nice ROI from properties that I sell outright. A 30-year loan modification isn't always in a borrower's best interests, so I may agree to an early discounted payoff in a lump sum, or just have the property signed over to me. Then I get the property up to standards and sell it for a profit, ideally.

I've gotten to know the markets in Indiana and Ohio from a first mortgage note perspective, as well as Florida, where I've had success with second mortgages. That's mainly due to the health of the economy there. There have been equity spikes on a wide variety of properties all throughout the state of Florida, which significantly improves my odds for high returns on investment.

Whatever the eventual outcome, I go into every note opportunity with the anticipation of making at least a 30% return on investment. If I'm not doing that, given the amount of risk, and given the number of variables that are outside my control, then it's not worth it for me to do. On average I am hitting at least that 30% mark.

That may seem high, but I can say from experience with my own portfolio, and portfolios I've worked on for my investors, that it is very achievable. This is really a knowledge-based business. You have to keep educating yourself. You have to keep being meticulous as you're working through notes, and if you do all the steps correctly, you will minimize that risk level. Someone with no experience who buys a note portfolio is going to have a higher risk level than mine. But risk can be drastically drops going forward as you continually learn about what you're doing and how to follow the right steps.

How have you helped both borrowers and the community as a whole?

I like that I'm able to give borrowers options that will benefit them as well as my bottom line. Communities have been hit hard by this recession that's lingered on for eight years. I've seen communities that have lost jobs, with factory jobs going overseas, leaving the town with vacant homes all around. If I can play my small part in helping borrowers get back on their feet with payments they can afford, or by taking back the properties and renting them out to people that can afford them, then I feel like I'm helping improve the health of their communities, as a whole.

When the borrower benefits, the whole community benefits. From a macro level, it doesn't look good to see the ugly "bandit signs," which some real estate investors use to promote their business in a neighborhood, where they're saying, "Call us and we'll buy your house for cash." Then a few houses down the street you see some boarded-up windows or lawns where the grass is two feet high, because the town doesn't have the revenue to cut the grass. If back taxes are owed on properties in the community, the county's not receiving revenue they need to provide services. And the borrowers are in hiding, because they know they can't afford to make payments. All those factors affect neighborhoods in a negative way, so there's less chance for growth or investment.

But if I can go in and really help these borrowers get caught up, well, guess what happens? They're going to take more pride in their home. They're going to have a sense of responsibility and do more to fix up the property. You won't see as many boarded windows, or overgrown lawns, and the counties will receive their tax dollars. So the quality of life in the community improves, and everyone benefits.

What are the various ways one can invest in the note business?

If all this sounds intriguing to you and you'd like to get involved in note investing, you have some options to fit your circumstances.

If you're not quite ready to go "full bore" as an investor, the best thing to do, assuming you have access to capital, is to reach out to an expert note investor. They may have partnership arrangements whereby people can come in on a passive level and witness how the note experience unfolds. They can stand at the investor's shoulder and watch what they're doing, then over time they might decide to try to do the full thing for themselves. That can be a great learning experience. Just make sure you vet the expert. You can receive help with vetting the expert at my Facebook group page Note Investing Made Easier.

Another passive option is that there are loan servicing companies that will do the full collections process for you. They have a loss mitigation option, where you pay extra per month and they'll make the phone calls and go through the whole legal process of foreclosure and borrower outreach. I haven't heard as many success stories with that option for folks, because normally these loan service companies have a large portfolio of loans that they're collecting on, so they tend to get bogged down with volume. They're also not as personally invested in the process as someone who just put out $20,000 to purchase a note and is working to see a return on that. They're coming from a different angle.

Of course, if you have the time and capital and want to put in the work and get your hands dirty, that's always welcomed in this industry. I always wish the best for anyone who wants an active role and goes through experiences similar to the ones I went through in order to be fully operational.

Whatever path you choose in the note investing industry, I recommend an upfront investment in your education. Much of what I learned in the industry was hands on and ended up costing me tens of thousands of dollars of hard lessons in the beginning. This is the reason I developed the online course "Note Investing Fundamentals".

I teach future note investors, how to:

- Create an action plan

- Source successfully in today's market

- Perform a 3-round due diligence process

- Use the right vendors for sourcing and due diligence

- Create ROI projections on notes before you buy

- Build a game plan post purchase and work with all the needed vendors

- Arrange and review our collateral file

- Have your assignments recorded

- Use servicing and achieve your exit strategy

- Portfolio management

The active investor

If you want to be actively involved in the process, are willing to get your hands dirty doing the workouts and getting up to speed from a knowledge standpoint, then be prepared for a fulltime commitment. Also, your capital has to withstand the test of time, because there are cases where you'll have notes that take longer to resolve.

Whether you're an active or passive investor, you need to expect to buy a portfolio of notes from the beginning. I run into investors who want to test the waters by buying just one note, but they won't get the full spectrum of experience that way.

Not every note performs. You could make a good percentage of return on one note, but then on the second one it's wiped out, and you'll feel discouraged.

For example, if you buy four notes, you may have one that you get crushed on, like if the house was stripped out after you bought the note. But then you may have two that are home runs and one that just maintains the current level for you.

Overall, it's a winning portfolio, but if you'd stopped at the first one you'd feel like a failure. So to get the true picture of how successful you can be with this, you really need to come out of the gate running with multiple notes.

If you're interested in jumping in, check out noteinvestingmadeeasier.com for tons of content.

Or you can email me directly at:

martin@2cfnow.com

CHAPTER 6

MANAGING YOUR PORTFOLIO

Rich people manage their money well.
Poor people mismanage their money well.

— *T. Harv Eker*

Throughout this book I've shared my best tips and processes involved in note investing, from researching and buying notes to working out exit strategies. In this final chapter I'm going to give you some details about systemizing your way to success, where you'll learn what to track and how. I'll expand on the topic of maintaining a good relationship with your loan servicer so you can get results. And I'll close by explaining how to get in touch with me to start creating ongoing profits for yourself and your family.

How to build systems that help optimize success

I am a methodical person and a big factor in my long-term success as a note investor has been my insistence on doing things systematically. These are the systems I recommend you have in place to manage your portfolio and stay on top of everything that's going on over time.

Managing collateral file data

The first thing you need to have prepared when you receive the collateral file for a note is some type of database system, where you can record all the pertinent information about that note, such as the borrower information - name, address, email address, phone number, etc.; what the interest rate of the note is; the last payment received; principal balance; and other key factors.

The online platform I use to capture all of that information is called Note Dashboard, and I highly recommend it. For a reasonable monthly fee you can document an unlimited number of notes. It's really easy to use, and it's a cloud-based system, so you can log on to it from anywhere. Another thing it does is uniformly displays information from note to note, so you're able to really understand what you have across the whole portfolio.

Tracking your borrower outreach

The second step is to create a system for tracking the workout of the note, starting with the welcome package that goes out to the borrowers. To refresh your memory, this is where you're introducing yourself, letting the borrowers know that you now own the note and that you're here to stay. After you send out the welcome letter, you'll continue tracking each step of the borrower outreach process, so you'll know when you're making x amount of calls and sending x amount of letters per week to the borrowers. Every time you're involved in a borrower outreach activity, it should be documented in a timeline format.

Tracking legal matters

The same goes for scheduling and tracking all the legal activity involved. You need a system in place to avoid delays so you can make efficient use of your time. Let's say you have an attorney send a Notice of Default letter to a borrower. There's most likely a 30-day window for a reply to that letter. You should be checking in with the attorney a day prior to the expiration date and getting the attorney prepared for the next steps. There's already time factored into the 30 days - the recording process, getting in touch with the borrower, etc. - so do yourself a favor and keep track of those documents in a database. Probably the worst thing you can do in this industry is waste time because it affects the amount of return you'll get over the life of a note.

Done-for-you systems

Those are just three of the most important systems you'll need to manage. There is a lot to stay on top of and it can be overwhelming if you don't take a structured approach. In Chapter 5 we talked about how average investors who partner with me may choose to stay out of all the detailed operations. The good news is if someone were to choose to work with me, all the systems I mentioned above, and more, are included in the service I provide for them.

I work out the notes for other investors using the same process and systems that I have for myself, with the notes that I own.

It would just be too complicated if I tried to deviate and have a separate system for each investor than I do for myself, because a lot of my activities are done in a grouping fashion. At a certain point of the week, I'll send out all my, and my clients', letters. At certain times of the day, I'll make all my, and my clients', phone calls, and so on. For me to have a different mindset or different approach for an investor than I would for myself would drive me insane. It wouldn't make any sense from an efficiency standpoint. I get better results from systematically working through one task at hand than switching back and forth multiple times a day.

Investing as an art form

While I'm talking about systems, I'd like to mention again that there is an art to this business. Even though there are concrete procedures and a lot of things are mapped out for you, it's not all science.

A lot of what I bring to the table in this industry is the ability to intuitively see things on a credit report that lead me to different strategies with different borrowers. For example, if I feel like I'm not making headway with phone calls, I may decide it's time to send a door knocker. From the credit report I know that the borrower works as a school teacher. So I would strategically schedule the door knocker to arrive at 5:30 pm, when the school teacher is most likely home.

Every note has its own life, so you have to use your judgment. It's really an art form to use different techniques with each borrower to get in touch with them. You'll have to master the art of dealing with the human side of investing.

The "nuts and bolts," impersonal, part of the note process happened at the origination stage, the underwriting process when the loan was initially given to the borrower.

If the borrower's application met certain parameters, the underwriter signed off, and the loan was granted. From that time to when those notes are bundled up and sold through the hedge funds and capital investment firms, it's only a numbers game. They don't delve into the borrowers' situations the way I do. They don't get their hands dirty and really connect with the borrower on a deep level. That's when the importance - and art - of understanding the human element kicks in.

How do you monitor your portfolio's performance?

Similar to stock market investors who have different ways to monitor the success of their portfolio, you as a note investor will have to monitor and measure the success of all the different types of notes in your portfolio, each with different parameters.

For the notes that are performing - in other words, the ones where you're getting payments from the borrower - the loan servicing companies send a monthly remittance report. It gives you a breakout of what's been paid toward principal on the note and what's paid toward interest. You can bounce that data off of your original projections and see how you're faring.

I keep updated profit and loss statements on all investor portfolios that I manage, as well as on mine. I consistently record purchase price, all the expenses, and all the income that's coming in on a monthly basis, so I'm able to see where things are each month. I recommend using QuickBooks to help you stay on top of everything. I use a website called Fiverr whereby you can outsource bookkeeping to handle all your record keeping needs. I find I get better service and significantly better pricing as I have my book reconciled quarterly to keep on track with all my financial activity. Come year end, I have my bookkeeper rolls the numbers up and I'm ready to file. I find I save a lot of money I used to pay my CPA and I'm more efficient than ever with record keeping.

Tips on managing your loan servicer

Talking about loan servicing companies and how they send monthly updates reminded me of some more insights you need to know about managing your relationship with loan servicers, making sure you're getting what you need from them.

When choosing a servicer, it's important that you interview and feel comfortable with the company, because you are going to be entering into a partnership relationship with them. You need to get that "warm and fuzzy" feeling in terms of what they'll provide for the money you'll be paying monthly.

Let's say that you've been introduced to the point of contact with Land Home Financial Services or FCI Lender Services. If you feel you have a good dialogue with them, and they make you feel comfortable, with no red flags, then I think that's a good indicator you've found a partner.

But keep in mind that everything's a two-way street. If you are giving the loan servicer half of the data they need to manage loans, if you're not responsive to them when they have issues that come up - like when the borrower phones in and says they can't make a payment, or if they have questions about ongoing maintenance of notes - then you're probably not going to have a good partnership with that loan servicer. They have thousands of notes that they're dealing with, and if you're not doing your part, then they're not going to make you a priority, just like what would occur in any other relationship in life.

If you want a job where you're getting fed tasks by a boss all day who tells you how to best perform, help them with their agenda and make them look good, then go do that. But in the note industry, from the relationships with borrowers and vendors you build, to the notes that you buy, all of the responsibility is on you. One hundred percent.

How can someone reach you and what can they expect when they do?

I hope that some of the things I've told you about note investing have piqued your interest and you'd like to know more. If you would like to reach out and begin a dialogue with me, the best way to start is to visit my website at noteinvestingmadeeasier.com. It gives you information about our company as well as the various options you have to work with me and my company.

If you're still at the information-gathering stage, the best thing to do is to get on Facebook and other social media and join the different note investing groups. You can post questions and there are a lot of note folks like myself who will chime in and build off each other's responses. That's a sure-fire way to get engaged and get started.

Unfortunately, I have time constraints. I have a family and I have a business operation, so I don't have a lot of time to spend with folks if they're not really ready to start working with me.

I'll do my best and look at all the responses that come in, anyway. But to save time, try to have your ducks in a row before contacting me directly. My wife will thank you

CASE STUDY 1:

FIRST MORTGAGE NOTE INVESTMENT IN DAYTON, OHIO

In the previous chapter Martin discussed several exit strategies note investors need to understand. He explained that the "Golden Rule" for note investing is to do a loan modification with the existing borrowers to help them get back on their feet and paying on the loan again.

In 2015 he found a note that turned out to be a winner because of his Golden Rule approach. In this case study we'll talk about where he found the note, how much he paid, the work out process, his contact with the borrowers and how it all ended up with a positive outcome.

Editor: How did you happen to find this note? How did it first come to your attention?

Martin Saenz: This was one of the first notes I ever purchased, and I got it through an online marketplace site called FCI (www.fciexchange. com), which is a popular and trustworthy source for notes.

Editor: You had mentioned in a previous chapter that FCI is a great source for note investors who are just getting started. This will be great example for those people since, in this case study, you were a new mortgage note investor yourself. What was the back story on this property? What sort of information did you examine, and what conclusions did you come to that led you to buy this note?

Martin Saenz: It was a first mortgage note related to a property in Dayton, Ohio. It was a good, strong, blue-collar area with modest crime and average schools. The fair market values of the properties around the neighborhood were between $40,000 and $60,000. So, it was slightly above the blighted property category. But that's the kind of profile I was looking for in a first mortgage pickup.

Editor: How far in arrears were their payments at the time?

Martin Saenz: They hadn't made a payment in about two and a half years. So, between late fees, interest, and other collection fees, they had arrears of around $20,000.

Editor: What was the mortgage principle balance as compared to the fair market value of the property?

Martin Saenz: They were underwater on the first mortgage when I ran across the note in 2015. At the time their principal balance was $90,000 and the fair market value of the property was between $50,000 and $55,000. They had purchased this property in 2006 at the height of the housing market, when values were inflated.

Editor: What was the price you paid for the note?

Martin Saenz: I purchased the note at $8,500, but I also knew there would be some work out costs.

Editor: I know you go through a due diligence process in examining these notes. What other things did you discover about the note, the property and the borrowers?

Martin Saenz: I checked into back taxes and found they owed $5,000. From the broker price opinion (BPO) report, which is where I send a realtor out to examine the property, take exterior photos and provide a list of comparable prices in the area, I found that the property was extremely well maintained. The borrowers had taken good care of the landscaping, and the siding and roofing looked new. I viewed them as people who really cared about the property, and if the exterior looked like that, it was probably a reflection of how the interior looked as well. It gave me the sense that these were people who would be motivated to stay in the home.

Editor: What did credit checks, background checks, etc. reveal to you about these borrowers?

Martin Saenz: The borrowers had modest income, yet they were very frugal in how they spent money. I found no extravagant lines of credit with car dealerships or expensive retailers. I concluded they probably had some kind of fixed income, or a lower-paying job, and were struggling financially, feeling the pressure of being behind on the payments and all the additional late fees. I believed they were good candidates for loan modification.

Editor: So they had bought more house than they could afford, then when the floor fell out of the market in 2008 they were caught between a rock and a hard place?

Martin Saenz: Absolutely. Yes.

Editor: Was there any other due diligence that you did or information up front that caused you to think that this would be a good note to invest in?

Martin Saenz: Yes, a couple of things. The title report came back showing that there was no second mortgage on the property. It had a clean tax lien status, so I just needed to pay back taxes. From my perspective, it was just a matter of purchasing a note associated with borrowers that really wanted to stay in their home, helping to position them where they could start making mortgage payments again.

Editor: Let's recap.

- The nominal amount of the mortgage was $90,000.
- The fair market value was $50,000-$55,000.
- It was about $20,000 in arrears, in penalties and so forth,
- and there were also $5,000 in unpaid property taxes.
- You paid $8,500 for the note.

Was that your original bid?

Martin Saenz: Yes. They accepted my first bid of $8,500 pretty quickly.

Editor: Okay, so now you're the proud owner of an underwater $90,000 mortgage, where payments haven't been made in over two years, but your goal is to turn it into a gem. What happened next?

Martin Saenz: I started a six-month long campaign of introducing myself and reaching out to the borrower so they would feel comfortable working with me. But I paralleled those efforts with legal activity to let the borrower know the seriousness of the situation.

Editor: It sounds like a "carrot and stick" campaign.

Martin Saenz: Yes. Borrowers need to understand the seriousness of it and that I mean business so that they'll take action. Otherwise they may feel like I'm coming on the scene for a while, but if they wait it out long enough, I'll move on in a few months, and then someone else is going to come along and replace me. Then they can kind of maintain the status quo, keep the cycle going. When I let them know through certain legal tactics as well as just good old fashioned phone calls and sending out welcome letter packages, this lets them know that I'm a professional and I'm here to stay.

Editor: How did you begin your dialogue with the borrowers, and how were you received?

Martin Saenz: It went pretty well. I called the borrower, and we had a nice conversation. I learned that they had lost their job for a few years. They had just recently gotten a new job that paid better than the one they'd lost. Financially, they were at a point when they were getting back on their feet. Couple that with the fact that they took good care of the property and loved where they lived, it was a positive sign. I sat down with them and worked out loan modification terms with that borrower.

Editor: What were the new terms?

Martin Saenz: I significantly reduced their principle balance to get it more in line with what the fair market value was. I reduced their interest rate, lowering their monthly payments based on what I understood they could afford. That gave them a sense of relief that they owned a home that they were going to be able pay off someday, instead of the hopeless feeling of owing twice as much as it's worth.

Editor: How did you handle paying the back taxes?

Martin Saenz: When you buy a first mortgage note you really have to prepare for paying the back taxes right away. Otherwise, liens could get placed on the property at very high interest rates, and you could lose the property to a tax lien note investor or the county. The county can place municipal liens against the property. You're protecting your asset by quickly paying those back taxes.

Editor: How long did it take before you were able to actually see some cash coming back to you from this note?

Martin Saenz: Within a few weeks of my initial dialogue with the borrower, we had a loan modification in place and I started seeing payments coming in within six months of purchasing the note.

Editor: How does the modification work? Did you draw up a new note with the new terms?

Martin Saenz: It's not a new note, but an extension of the existing note that notates the changes of terms.

Editor: So you picked up the note in 2015. Are the borrowers continuing to make payments? Are you still servicing this note? What's your exit strategy?

Martin Saenz: That note paid per the terms of the loan modification for about 16 months, and then I sold that note on the same online website where I'd purchased the original.

Editor: Can you give us an idea of your profits on this note?

Martin Saenz: I bought it for $8,500 and put about $7,500 of work out expenses into it, so about $16,000 all in. While the note was seasoning I received $7,200 in monthly payments and then sold the note for $37,000.

Editor: That's awesome. With six months of work out time and 16 months of payments, that's 22 months. And over that period of time you turned a $16,000 investment into $44,200 in returns. Very impressive.

Martin Saenz: Yes, it was favorable.

Editor: That's an excellent case study. Is there anything else you can share with us that you learned from your experience with this note?

Martin Saenz: Not trying to pat myself on the back, and I know I've said this before, but it really warms my heart that I was able to help the borrowers and significantly reduce the debt on the property and allow them to get back on their feet. On top of making a few dollars in the process, it's just a really good feeling when you can help somebody out of a jam.

Editor: You helped them to have a feeling like there's light at the end of the tunnel.

Martin Saenz: Absolutely, and given there have been equity spikes across the country, I'd guess the fair market value at least matches what they owe at this point, so that puts them in an even better position, so that makes me happy.

CASE STUDY 2:

FIRST MORTGAGE NOTE INVESTMENT IN TIRO, OHIO

When you buy 1st non-performing mortgage notes, your focus is on the property. This was Martin's first note he purchased and he bought it through the online marketplace called FCI Exchange in early 2014.

Editor: Why did you select this note as your first note to purchase?

Martin Saenz: For this note and 9 other notes I initially purchased, they were all located in the state of Ohio. I really like the blue collar feel within Ohio and how the state has been progressing from a growth standpoint. Plus, there was an abundance of inventory in the state at the time. So, I went on a road trip across Ohio to view this property and others around Ohio. Tiro OH is a rural area north of Mansfield and I found it to have a pretty country feel to it. The house sat on about an acre and looked to be vacant.

Editor: How much did you pay for the note?

Martin Saenz: I paid $10,500 for the note and $3,000 was owed in back taxes. Thus, my total all in to buy the note was $13,500 and the borrower owed 99k.

Editor: You would think a vacant property would scare an investor. How did you see the opportunity with the note?

Martin Saenz: There is always risk with a vacant property. It can be stripped out with all the plumbing and guts. Without having access to go inside, you really have to rely on judgment based on what you see from the outside. In this case, the property looked slightly run down but it still captured a decent looking country home that sat on an acre of land. I felt the borrower has moved on from the property and I could approach him for a deed in lieu to help him get past his past. Also, I was buying the note at such a low price knowing the property would fetch for 30k to 40k.

Editor: How did it go reaching out to the borrower?

Martin Saenz: After 2 months, I reached the borrower and he immediately signed over the property via deed in lieu in exchange for me forgiving all his debt obligation. You see, when I purchased the note, I assumed all the rights of the original lender so he owed me the full balance of 99k. The borrower jumped at the opportunity to be forgiven of a 99k burden since he had moved on in life mentally and physically.

Editor: You have the deed in lieu, now what?

Martin Saenz: My strategy is always to do as little as possible financially and physically to get the property positioned for resell. I relied on a national repair service to cut the lawn and resold the property for 36k after 5 months of note ownership. The couple that bought the property was a retired couple and they put down 18k towards the 36k purchase. I took back a seller takeback note for 18k at 7% interest over 8 years. This gives me monthly payments of $245.

Editor: That is a wild turn of events. Where you nervous about how it would play out given it was your first note purchase?

Martin Saenz: Yes, it was really crazy. My intension is always to opt for the ongoing cash flow through a loan modification, but with this note I had expected to do a quick flip for capital gains. It turned out to hold both a capital gains and cash flow component. In hindsight there are several reasons why I may not buy this property as I'm investing today. For one, I stay away for very rural areas whereby there is limited access to jobs. Second, since my objective is always cash flow, I look for notes whereby it's the borrower's primary residence. In this case it turned out well, however I would not make buying this type of note part of my buying model.

Editor: That is awesome. You buy the note for $13,500, connect with the borrower for a deed in lieu, and resell the property for $36,000 5 months later. As part of the resell, you receive a seller takeback note for $18,000 at 7% interest over 8 years paying you $245 monthly.

CASE STUDY 3:

SECOND MORTGAGE NOTE INVESTMENT IN PALM BAY, FLORIDA

Editor: We're going to dive into the details of a second mortgage note opportunity that Martin opted to buy in Palm Bay, Florida. This case study will give some insight into the differences between buying a first and second mortgage note, as well as the importance of knowing the territory where the property is located. Let's start from the beginning.

Editor: Where did you find this note?

Martin Saenz: I found it through a peer note seller who was looking to liquidate and sell off the note, so it wasn't out on the street for everyone to see. This note was part of a tape portfolio of five notes total, but this is the one that stood out to me.

Editor: What was the status of this note when it came to your attention? After your three rounds of due diligence regarding the note, the property and the buyers, what gave you the feeling that you could turn this note around and turn it into a performing note?

Martin Saenz: The principal balance was at $44,500 dollars. The borrower had not made a payment on this second mortgage in about four years, so there was a great deal of interest arrears and late fees that had accumulated on that note.

I looked into the first mortgage and found the payments and taxes were current. The balance on the first mortgage was about $130,000 and the property was worth about $160,000.

One of the things that really intrigued me about this note was that I knew $160,000 would not remain $160,000 for very long. I'm a big fan of buying notes in Florida because they've had a series of equity spikes over the last few years. So I had forecast that the property value in that area was on the rise.

The borrowers were self-employed and owned several businesses. Being self-employed myself, I felt I would be able to connect with them on that level. Since I'd already found they were paying on their first mortgage, I felt that they had emotional equity and probably wanted to stay in the home.

I'd gotten a broker price opinion (BPO) report, which means a realtor went out, took exterior photos of the property and provided a list of comparable properties in the area. I found that the landscaping was in excellent condition and the borrower was taking good care of the property.

Since they also were diligently paying on their first mortgage, this told me that, more than likely, they just had some dire circumstance in their life that hindered their ability to pay on the second mortgage. The credit report confirmed they were fairly conservative with their money and didn't have much outstanding debt.

I didn't have any specific information as to why they had continued to pay their first mortgage but stopped paying their second mortgage for four years. Normally when that happens, there's some type of crisis situation involved, like a divorce, or a serious health issue that came up suddenly. Once borrowers start to fall behind, it almost becomes easier to just ignore it and hope that by staying current on the first mortgage they won't have to go into foreclosure.

Part of the problem in these cases is that larger banking institutions or hedge funds don't know how to connect with borrowers. They don't work out terms with them to get them back on track. It's not their line of business, plus they're limited by regulations that prevent them from being flexible with the borrowers. When the borrowers see the rigidness of that lender, they just go into hibernation.

Editor: So had you purchased the note from an individual investor or a larger organization?

Martin Saenz: An individual who's a slightly larger player, like one notch up from me. They buy in bigger bulk from hedge funds and capital investment firms, so oftentimes when they're selling me a mortgage note they've doubled that original note price, which doubles their money on that sale to me. They're more inclined to do that because they want to offload quickly and recapitalize—let me to do the dirty work.

Editor: As we discussed earlier, the principle balance was $44,500. How much did you end up paying for this note?

Martin Saenz: I purchased it at $3,600. But that was in 2014. You might pay $9,600 for a similar opportunity in that area of Florida today. But, when you see how things were resolved with this note, you would gladly entertain the $9,600 opportunity. Even though note prices are increasing, it's really where the numbers lie at the end of the deal that determine your ROI. So a higher-priced note can still be very attractive.

Editor: Tell us about the workout process. Were you able to get a dialogue going with the borrower?

Martin Saenz: Yes, we worked together over a period of time to come up with an agreement. It took about 16 months for resolution to occur, which ended up being a loan modification. I spent about $6,600 dollars in legal expenses and some other collection expenses. I did press the borrower on foreclosure, and at about the 12 month mark they actually filed bankruptcy, which was a good thing in this case because there was equity in the property.

The state of Florida has mediation programs available to the borrower, which are awesome for note investors, because the mediator oftentimes helps move the loan modification along. I find that these modifications are more sustainable and end up being successful because the state mediators and the borrowers' legal counsel hash out the details. So I welcomed the state's mediation program's involvement in this transaction.

We were able to work out a loan modification over a three-month period. The borrowers reduced their payment by about $200 per month and their interest rate was lowered to 10-1/2% over a 30-year fixed period, which helped the borrower get back on track with their payments.

Editor: Are you still holding the note?

Martin Saenz: I kept the note for about a year after the loan modification began and then sold it for $28,000.

Editor: So let me recap. You had:

- $3,600 for the purchase price
- $6,600 in workout expenses

- About $4,800 in payments for the 12 months you held the note
- A selling price of $28,000
- For a net of about $22,600 over a 28-month period

Editor: You made an excellent return on that note!

In addition to the benefit of recapturing some of your workout expenses, do you hold the note for a certain period of time to prove that it's performing again before you go out and sell it?

Martin Saenz: It's true—the more seasoned the note, the more value. I like to get at least get a year of seasoning with a note before I sell it. But sometimes I keep the notes indefinitely and, in some cases, I'm buying notes through my self-directed IRA, so they will just remain in my portfolio for years to come.

Editor: Would you share what type of buyer you sold this note to?

Martin Saenz: It's someone I have built a very good trust relationship with. I know I can turn to them with an opportunity and within 24 hours have an agreement and money transferred. This investor has ample capital and has a long-term strategy of buying seasoned notes and holding on to them.

Editor: What else do we need to know about this note opportunity?

Martin Saenz: I want to stress how important it is to know the territories where you're buying these notes. From the time I bought this note until the time I sold it, the fair market value of the property increased by $60,000. So my expenses were covered, equity wise, and the note just got prettier over time, as I anticipated. That was Florida. But the flip side can also happen. You can also see depressed areas, where factories have closed down or are getting ready to move operations to another country. Those areas are having a really hard time as jobs are eliminated. So these are things to consider as part of your due diligence in deciding whether to purchase a note in the first place.

CASE STUDY 4:

FIRST MORTGAGE NOTE INVESTMENT IN HOUTZDALE, PA

This is an example of how building good relationships with sellers pays off. Martin spent time cultivating a relationship with a fellow peer out of Florida. The seller happened to be in need of recapitalizing so he offered Martin an 'off the street' opportunity to pick up several of his notes at solid wholesale pricing. There is something to be said with establishing yourself as someone who can close quickly and does what they say they will do.

In this case Martin picked up a 1st mortgage note on a vacant property in the State College area. He paid $10,000 for the note and the borrower owed $50,000. The property was worth within a range of $30,000 to $60,000 depending on how the inside fared.

Editor: How do you value such a property when purchasing this note?

Martin Saenz: Generally, I look at the fair market value of the property compared to the amount of expenses involved, such as back taxes, municipal fines, forced place insurance, servicing costs, and projected legal fees. In this case, I received a Broker's Price Opinion report which gave me information on a recommend price, exterior pictures, other property comparisons, and the overall market trend for that area.

Regarding the risk with this vacant property, there is always the chance that if the borrower does not want to cooperate, I would have to burn a lot of time and money going through the foreclosure process in a judicial state like Pennsylvania.

All in all, I looked at a fair market value of 35k against 16k of expenses.

Editor: How did this note play out with the borrower?

Martin Saenz: I made contact with the borrower in about 3 months and he was anxious to sign over the property. It turned out, he had gone through a divorce and left the property given the bad feelings involved. He was always worried about the debt on the property and was relieved that I would forgive his debt in exchange for him signing over a property he resented. You could say I made his day if not year.

Editor: What happened to the property from that point?

Martin Saenz: I got the lawn cut and the property winterized, and signed up with a realtor to resell the property. In about 4 months, I had a contract for $31,000 to buy the property with a seller takeback option. The terms were $31,000 balance at 4.675% over 10 years for monthly payments of $323 per month. You can call that interest rate a veteran special as the buyer was a U.S. military veteran that purchased the property with the intention of living there while rehabbing it. Today, the borrower lives in the property and has it all fixed up. I'd say the fair market value is around $70,000 as I write this.

Editor: Take me through the WIN WIN business model you often talk about?

Martin Saenz: In this case, I'd say it was an exponential WIN for every party involved. For one, the note seller got to recapitalize by quickly off-loading the note to myself, I win by profiting with a $31,000 mortgage note for roughly $13,000 in cost, the borrower gets past a heavy debt burden, the veteran receives a home at a favorable rate, and the community has a vacant property removed from its neighborhood.

Editor: You have mentioned that you do not like to buy vacant properties especially in rural areas, yet you made this work once again. Do you think you would perhaps change your model to look for these properties?

Martin Saenz: To be honest, if you are focusing on building the right relationships, good wholesale opportunities will come your way. There are plenty of notes out there that are located in good job growth areas that you don't have to take chances in rural communities. With that said, if an opportunity presents itself and you are receiving very favorable pricing given your vetted projected returns, you have to follow the deal.

CASE STUDY 5:

SECOND MORTGAGE NOTE INVESTMENT IN MOUNT PLEASANT, SOUTH CAROLINA

Editor: Now it's time to look at case study involving a note Martin Saenz purchased for a property in Mount Pleasant, South Carolina. I believe it was a second mortgage note, correct?

Martin Saenz: That's correct.

Editor: I'd like to go through the whole process with you, chronologically. First off, how did you find this note? How did it come to your attention?

Martin Saenz: It was a peer note investor who was offloading some notes. I met them at a conference, and they sent me over the opportunity.

Editor: Was this part of a tape, a group of notes, or were you able to buy it on its own?

Martin Saenz: It was part of a tape, but I was able to cherry pick the ones I wanted. I bought five or six notes from that tape.

Editor: I know that you are a very thorough investigator and you have three rounds of due diligence on every note that you consider investing in. You don't have to go through every detail, but as you were doing your due diligence on this particular note, and this property, what was it about this situation that gave you the feeling you could get this thing turned around and turn it into a winner?

Martin Saenz: I thought there was good equity there. The property was valued at about $220k and the first mortgage was current. There was no issue with back taxes. The first mortgage note had a principle balance of about $153,000, so there was slightly under $70,000 in equity. I felt that was a good number to play with.

Editor: What was the unpaid principle balance on the second mortgage?

Martin Saenz: $37,000

Editor: How long had it been since they'd made a payment on it?

Martin Saenz: Between three and four years.

Editor: It's still amazing to me that people go that many years without making a payment and are still living in the house.

Martin Saenz: I've seen much worse. Three to four years is the norm.

Editor: Amazing. I assume that means they'd also been paying their insurance as part of their PITI—principle, interest, taxes and insurance—on their first mortgage.

Martin Saenz: The insurance is handled a little differently on a second mortgage note. If the first mortgage doesn't have verification of insurance on file for the property, many times the first mortgage lender will pay for force-placed insurance. They will later recoup that money from the borrowers, themselves, not from me. That's an expense the first mortgage note owner has to deal with. Meanwhile, what that actually does is it protects my asset in my second mortgage stand.

Editor: I'm sure you appreciate that.

Martin Saenz: Absolutely. Very much so.

Editor: How far in arrears were they in interest, penalties and so forth?

Martin Saenz: Right around $18,000 in arrears.

Editor: Wow! So the situation was a $37,000 unpaid principle second mortgage balance that hadn't been paid in three to four years, with $18,000 in arrears. What was the purchase price that you and the seller agreed to on this note?

Martin Saenz: $2,526 is what I paid for the note.

Editor: I know you generally have an estimated amount of work out costs you expect to pay. What amount did you have in mind when you bought this note?

Martin Saenz: Since it was a second mortgage and everything looked pretty cut and dried with it, I expected about $4,000 to spend with legal costs to work out that note.

Editor: We'll reveal later what you actually ended up paying. Next I wanted to ask you about the borrower. I know you have a systematic way of reaching out to borrowers. This particular case seems like someone who had been dodging lenders for quite some time. What steps did you take to get in touch with this person? How were you able to make a connection and actually communicate with the borrower?

Martin Saenz: I first tried calling. I had a good phone number for the borrower. She was an older lady, a retired civil servant. I made sure to call at all different times of day to try to see what her schedule was like. But I was never able to get in touch with her.

So we initiated the foreclosure process. We filed the complaint. And about midway through the process, at about 10 to 12 months into the foreclosure, we were notified that the borrower had retained an attorney and wanted to go through a loan modification. That's when communication with the borrower began. But I never spoke to her. Everything was done through the legal teams at that point.

Editor: You've explained before that your preference is always to speak to the borrower directly, and personally. That means lower costs for you, because things can get resolved faster, which means you're able to work out a better deal for them.

In this particular case, was her lawyer trying to play hardball with you, making things more difficult? Or were you just thankful that there was someone you could talk to to get things moving?

Martin Saenz: The lawyer and I did have some positive conversations. I thought they were a really helpful and supportive law firm. You don't always get that. Sometimes you get the lawyers that just want to push certain issues to drag things out for the money. Or they try to push borrowers into bankruptcy when they clearly don't need to do that. But this attorney was responsive and really wanted to help out the borrower by getting this loan modification done, which is what we did.

Editor: We discussed earlier what the original status of the note was. After the loan modification process, what were the new terms?

Martin Saenz: We reset the principle balance at $36,000 and lowered the interest rate from about 9% to 6.13% on a 30 year fixed loan. This added up to monthly payments of $224, down from around $350 per month.

Editor: What about the arrears?

Martin Saenz: I forgave most of what was owed in arrears.

Editor: I'll bet that most borrowers would never believe that if they actually got on the phone with you, that you could cause $18,000 of arrears to go away, lower their monthly payment by a third, drop the interest rate significantly, and all you want to do is talk to them and get them back on track.

Martin Saenz: No doubt. If they only knew! But through my communications that I send out, my borrower outreach package, I do try to relay that. Obviously I can't promise an iron clad deal if I don't have a dialogue going on with them. But I do try to get it across in my communications that as this thing drags out, costs do incur and add up. I explain that the time to act is now, that I just want to have a conversation and figure out a way to help them out. It doesn't matter how bad they think things are, it would be better for them to work with me.

Editor: So from the day you purchased the note until it began performing again after the loan modification, how much time had elapsed?

Marting Saenz: It was about 14-15 months. The loan modification itself took quite a bit of time, three or four months.

Editor: What was it about this negotiation that made it take so long? Was it because of the communication through three parties?

Martin Saenz: It took about 45 days just to get her loss mitigation package, which is basically a request for her financial information. We request for her to fill out an application similar to the one she filled out when she got the mortgage in the first place. It's kind of a lengthy process, and she was an older lady, so perhaps she needed more help getting around. And when there are attorneys involved, you have to grant that time period, even when both sides are eager to get a loan modification done. So that was 45 days, and then it took another couple months to work out the loan modification. You just have to accept that it takes that much time. It is what it is.

Editor: What was the outcome in terms of your investment in this note? Did you allow it to season, as you say, for 12 months or more, where the borrower was making payments on it? Is it still in your portfolio, or did you sell it?

Martin Saenz: I sold this note. I had let it season for 18 months, and the borrower made on-time payments every month.

Editor: Before you tell us how much you sold it for, after estimating $4,000 in workout expenses, how much did it end up costing you?

Martin Saenz: $5,500. I had purchased it for around $2,500, plus the work out for $5,500 so about $8,000, all in.

Editor: So those legal costs really did add up. What did you sell it for?

Martin Saenz: I sold it for $15,000.

Editor: That's an excellent return. So in a little more than two years you turned $8,000 into $15,000.

Martin Saenz: Yes.

Editor: Do you have any closing thoughts about what we can learn from this case study?

Martin Saenz: What you learn when you have a win like this is that when you buy right and you work it out, and you season the note, then you sell it off for a good amount of profit, you just want to do it again. And again. And again. Rinse, and repeat.

CASE STUDY 6:

FIRST MORTGAGE NOTE INVESTMENT IN EUCLID, OHIO

In this case study we see how Martin's due diligence can find a hidden gem that might have looked like a risky investment at first blush. We also learn how building a relationship with the borrowers and having an attitude of service can turn things around in a big way, with a financial, and even an emotional, payoff for everyone involved.

Editor: Tell us about the property behind this note.

Martin Saenz: I bought this first mortgage note on a property in Euclid, Ohio - a suburb of Cleveland - from FCI (fciexchange. com) after my initial research showed it had potential.

Editor: What was it that piqued your interest about this particular note? What did your first round of due diligence show you that made you decide to jump on this opportunity?

Martin Saenz: This area of Cleveland is a good, working-class neighborhood, so what piqued my interest was the low initial cost of the note in what appeared to be a stable community.

Editor: What was the principal balance on this note?

Martin Saenz: The principal balance on the note was right at $30,000.

Editor: What was the fair market value of the property?

Martin Saenz: It was close to $24,000, so they were significantly underwater on this note.

Editor: How far in arrears were they? How long had it been since they'd made a mortgage payment?

Martin Saenz: It had been about three years since they had made a mortgage payment, and they owed back taxes as well. They were about $8,500 in arrears.

Editor: What made you feel as though this was a note you could get turned around?

Martin Saenz: First off, the price was right. I bought the note for only $3,500, so it was clear that the seller was really motivated to unload it. I knew there could be some risk to taking on this kind of property, because with a fair market value of $24,000 there's a good chance it's a blighted property, possibly in a high-crime area. The house could have been vacant, stripped out, and worth $5,000 at the end of the day.

However, this is where my due diligence helped me. I had a broker price opinion (BPO) done, where a realtor went to the property and took some pictures so I had a better idea of what I was dealing with. I found that the house had a car in the driveway, and the windows, siding and roofing looked to be in decent condition. It looked like a family lived there who cared for the property. So they probably had some level of emotional investment.

Editor: I know another part of your due diligence is to look at the borrowers themselves. Was there any information that you found about them that gave you a positive feeling?

Martin Saenz: Not at that point. I went into it just knowing what the back taxes were that I'd have to pay, knowing what the fair market value was and understanding about the liens on the property. I felt that gave me an understanding of where things stood with that note.

Editor: After you purchased the note, you then began to reach out and establish communication with the borrowers. What did you learn about their situation?

Martin Saenz: I found that the owner was a middle-aged woman who had gone through a series of issues with substance abuse and job losses and had been distant from her family and the property for quite some time. Her adult children were living in the home. It was the house they had grown up in, so it's what they'd known all their lives and were comfortable with. They very much wanted to stay in the house. This was a blessing, because I knew I had something to work with. They're paying the electric bill. They're taking care of the lawn. There must be money coming in from somewhere. That's when you put on your detective hat and really try to understand where they're at and strategize what can be done to help them in their situation.

Editor: How did you get the dialogue started, and how did the family feel about your involvement?

Martin Saenz: In this case, going through the foreclosure process got me in communication with Cuyahoga County. They have a mediation program in place there. I love the mediation programs because they always serve to bring the borrowers around to terms. So I was optimistic. A magistrate oversaw the process. The daughter of the woman who owned the property was the bookkeeper, and she got involved with knowing the numbers and understanding how things would be worked out, because she was the one who was taking on responsibility for the mortgage payments.

After working with her and the mediators, I ended up forgiving the arrears for a small upfront payment. I paid the back taxes and created a new mortgage note at the original $30,000 principal balance, but with a lower interest rate. This lowered the monthly payments and made them affordable.

The borrowers felt good about getting it back on track. The county mediators blessed it, because they saw we were making a concerted effort to help the family.

Editor: I can imagine the relief these people must feel. I bet there's an element of surprise when they realize you're actually trying to make this work for everyone. Do you ever have people say they are surprised that you are actually trying to help them?

Martin Saenz: All the time! Probably the greatest compliment is when I call them on the phone and they pick up and talk to me like someone they've known for years. Or they might send me a text to let me know, "Hey, I'm going to be a few days late this month with a payment." That tells me that they're engaged and feel committed to making the payment plan work. I've even gotten Christmas cards and texts with smiley face emojis. There are various ways I can see people's gratitude.

Giving people payments they can afford while at the same time making a healthy profit—there's no better investment that I'd want to be a part of than that.

Editor: How did this Euclid investment play out, in the end?

Martin Saenz: I received payments for about a year and a half. So $350 x 18 months was $6,300. That goes toward the expenses I had on that note, which were the initial $3,500 cost of the note plus the $6,000 work out cost, so $9,500 all in. Then I sold the note for $18,500.

Editor: That was a big transformation, from a $3,500 note to one for which someone was willing pay $18,500. I really appreciate your transparency about these transactions. It shows people that if you go about doing things the right way, this business can generate very substantial returns.

CASE STUDY 7:

SECOND MORTGAGE NOTE INVESTMENT IN RICHMOND, VA

Martin buys notes through his self-directed IRA and uses a company called IRA Services Trust Company. This allows Martin and his wife to take advantage of tax deferment on income received from notes. In this case, Martin purchased a performing 2nd mortgage note.

There are a number of requirements you have to know and follow to ensure you stay compliant with your IRA, otherwise you can open yourself up to various penalties. Buying notes through entities such as LLC's and S-Corps or through a self-directed IRA should be part of an overall portfolio management strategy. In other words, when you are done with running due diligence on the note opportunity, you should be able to quickly assess which entity type to buy the note under.

Editor: You normally buy non-performing notes at discounts, so why buy this performing note and how did you find the note?

Martin Saenz: Yes, my focus is on buying non-performing notes at deep discounts and getting those notes to perform for cash flow. In this case, I purchased 2 performing notes from a peer that was needing to recapitalize and this is a case study on 1 of the 2 notes. I got a sweet deal on this note as you will understand in just a moment. The note is on a property located in Richmond VA in a very nice suburb area and the borrower has good stable income.

The home is all around brick and the exterior appearance shows well. The current note terms are: $23,400 principal balance at 14.99% interest over the course of 27 xh remaining years. Monthly payments come to $297 and there is an arrears lump sum amount of $44,783 that will balloon upon payoff of the note. I paid $17,784.

Editor: That sounds like an amazing deal. Are there lots of these types of deals in the marketplace? What can new note investors expect when they start buying notes?

Martin Saenz: For one, I bought 2 similar notes from a peer I had a good relationship with. The more you network and transact amongst your peers, the more opportunities you will see. The seller could have posted this opportunity on one of the online exchanges but that would not have lead to money being wired into their account next day. The WIN WIN business model again is where everyone wins including the seller as they got what they needed which was fast money.

The key to focus on here is that for $17,784, my IRA is going to grow $297 per month over 27 xh years and then it will be set to receive a balloon payment of $44,783. If I went pounding the pavement for these types of deals, I would be hard pressed to find many of them. The idea is to be of service to your peers and be someone they look to for various matters. The deals will flow naturally from that.

Editor: You have to think at this point why more real estate investors are not jumping at these types of opportunities. Why is that?

Martin Saenz: It is because they don't understand our industry and there is no sexiness behind it. You find home rehabbing television shows all over whereby a young buck with six pack abs is swinging a hammer and the homeowner gets top dollar for their home at the end of the show. People are drawn to the sensationalism and it becomes real because it is being viewed right before their eyes. When you talk to the average Joe or even a real estate investor about notes, you can see their struggle with visualizing the process. It comes off as very convoluted and risky. Investors like to see physical properties because they are into control. They like to use their senses in examining the property. They want to know how does the roof, windows, HVAC, electrical, plumbing, etc. look? That is why most investors invest locally so they can camp out in their cars and watch the neighborhood and physically touch the property.

In some respect folks in the note industry benefit from complexity as it discourages many investors from entering the space. As for control, we operate like a banker by using trusted vendors to gather information on the property and borrower, and then to conduct an analysis based on the data. What most non-note investors do not really understand is that once we conduct our analysis we all visualize a picture of the borrower and property from the opportunity without ever leaving our home office. Thus, in a sense, we use our empirical senses.

Editor: Why write this book and bring light to this industry if it almost seems to benefit you from simply going about your business?

Martin Saenz: It because I feel a spiritual calling to help my fellow man find new opportunities to grow their finances. It is sad to me that most people throw their money into mutual funds and allow people they will never meet run their accounts.

Note investing is something that the investor can take full ownership of and can experience nice returns if done correctly.

CASE STUDY 8:

SECOND MORTGAGE NOTE INVESTMENT IN POMPANO BEACH, FLORIDA

Occasionally, note investors run into difficult characters who throw a wrench into the process. Investors need to understand the tools available to them and what "hot buttons" to push to motivate unruly borrowers into action. In this case study, Martin Saenz explains how he dealt with one borrower who became angry, even aggressive, when Martin began to establish communications with him and how he was able to turn the investment around for a nice profit.

Editor: This case study took place in Pompano Beach, Florida, where you invested in a distressed second mortgage note. Let's start from the beginning. How did you find this note? How did it come to your attention, initially?

Martin Saenz: A peer in the note industry who I know very well was off-loading some notes, and I picked it up as one in a portfolio of five notes.

Editor: I've noticed that the first notes you told us about were purchased on an online marketplace, but increasingly you're buying notes from peers that you've met in the industry. Is that a correct observation?

Martin Saenz: Absolutely. When I first started buying notes, I relied a lot on the FCI Exchange. They have a great platform.

The service is top-notch, which is helpful as you're going through the process, especially when you're learning. However, there is one thing to note. It's a retail setting, so prices tend to be higher. As you become a more seasoned investor, you can start picking up notes on a wholesale level, peer to peer, and getting in with small banks or investment firms. That's when you'll see a better price tag on the notes that you're buying.

Editor: As you've explained before, you've been able to do that because you've gotten involved with online platforms, bulletin boards, Facebook groups, note investing conferences, etc.

Martin Saenz: You have to put in the work in building the relationships, but once that happens and people trust you, then more valuable opportunities will open up for you in the note industry.

Editor: Going back to the Pompano Beach note—let's talk specifics. What was the unpaid balance on this note?

Martin Saenz: It had an unpaid principal balance of $42,000 when the note was bought.

Editor: How much was there in arrears?

Martin Saenz: They hadn't made a payment in six or seven years, so they owed about $30,000 in arrears.

Editor: To the uninitiated person like myself, that doesn't sound like a great investment bargain, but you, looking with your expert eye, saw potential in it. What was it that you saw that made it attractive enough to purchase?

Martin Saenz: First off, it's in Florida, and I always have an eye out for properties in Florida. I think it's a great state to buy notes in. And second, the borrowers were current on their first mortgage and there were no back taxes, so I felt like there was something there that I could work with.

Editor: After you negotiated with your peer, what price did you end up paying for this $42,000 note?

Martin Saenz: $5,000.

Editor: Then, as you always do, you started the process of getting things in order, which included reaching out to the borrower. That seems to me to be one of the most difficult aspects of what you do. How did you to try to communicate with them?

Martin Saenz: Through the skip trace report, I had a good phone number for the borrower, so I called them up. It didn't go so well. Initially, they cussed me out and threatened me, tried to give me the line that they didn't owe me any money.

I thought it was really an act of aggression to get me to back off, hoping I would go away. I knew I would have to take some serious steps to press the matter.

Editor: I've never heard you talk about an encounter like this one. How frequently does that kind of thing happen?

Martin Saenz: I'd say about 10% of the time you run into someone that's really angry and aggressive like that. It is very much part of the business. You have to be able to stomach tough phone calls, where people may despise you. But it's not you, personally, just who you represent and that you are forcing them to deal with this obligation they've put in the closet.

Editor: Once that borrower set a negative tone for your communication, how did you prepare to deal with them, going forward? What did you do?

Martin Saenz: The first thing I had to do was gather as much information about the borrower and the property as I could. It turned out that there was a renter living at the property, a tenant-filled property. The owner lived in northern Virginia and owned a government contracting company, working with the federal government. This person was far-removed from Florida and was comfortably taking rent payments from the tenant down there. It looked as though the borrower had money, so I knew I had some tactics I could use to get him back on track.

Editor: What tactics did you use?

Martin Saenz: I set up loan servicing, with the assurance that they would start reporting the borrower's failure to pay to the credit reporting agencies. I recognized his sensitive spot would be his business. He was working with federal government clients, and it wouldn't look good for him to have a property he hadn't made payments on in seven years. The credit reporting aspect was the key. That got his attention. His attorney reached out to my attorney and said, "We'll give you $9,000 to go away."

Editor: What was your response to that offer?

Martin Saenz: I said, "No way." That was totally unacceptable. This was not somebody who was struggling, financially. He lived in a half a million dollar home in a wealthy, northern Virginia county, and owned a successful government contracting business. He had been collecting rent from the tenants at this property for years and yet not paying his obligations for six or seven years. Money needed to be paid to rectify this situation.

Editor: Did this negotiation come down to a question of how big of a check he was going to have to pay to be released from his obligation?

Martin Saenz: Yes, after I started with the credit reporting, I notified the borrower's attorney to let them know that it was going to start showing up on the credit report and how far past due the payments were. That's when they sent another offer. They countered their offer at $25,000. I did accept that offer.

Editor: How much time had passed from the time you purchased the note until they made that $25,000 offer and you accepted it?

Martin Saenz: 16 months.

Editor: You had purchased the note for $5,000. Originally it was a $42,000 principle balance with about $30,000 in arrears, correct?

Martin Saenz: Yes.

Editor: How much work out costs did you put into this?

Martin Saenz: $6,000, so with the purchase price, that was $11,000, all in. The borrower paid an early discounted payoff of $25,000 to be released from the debt obligation and have a lien removed from the property.

Editor: So you more than doubled your money in 16 months. That's a significant return on investment.

Martin Saenz: I was happy about that, but I was also relieved it worked out so well, because this person was very difficult and aggressive toward me. It felt good to have the win and to get it off my desk.

There was another aspect to this that's important to understand, which is that there was no equity backing my position when I purchased the note.

Editor: What do you mean by that?

Martin Saenz: In other words, they were upside down on their first mortgage. Let's say the principal balance was around $250,000, and the property value was $170,000. When I buy a second mortgage note with $70,000 worth of debt, if there was a default on the first mortgage, then I would be wiped out and wouldn't see a penny.

New investors, and certain types of note investors, shy away from notes that have no equity supporting them on the second position. They want to stay with something comfortable, so they focus on real estate. What's the real estate? Is there equity backing my position? What's the property like? All the books they've read on real estate investing push the idea of equity first.

But certain boutique players, like myself, in the second mortgage arena focus on the borrowers' profiles. We look at emotional equity and take other factors into consideration. The reason for that is because if there's equity, you're going to pay top dollar for that note. I want to avoid paying an arm and a leg for a note, so the real art is finding a note where I feel the borrower can pay. Then I work to get them back to the table. That's my objective and mindset.

Editor: That's a great point. Again, it comes down to your talent in working with people one-on-one and understanding a person's hot button. That's where you really make your money. But even though you had this tremendous, more than 100% return, you clearly also had a pretty high level of risk, since you had no equity to back you.

Martin Saenz: That's right. Going into this, I didn't know if the borrower wanted to drag things out for three years by contesting everything imaginable, doubling my legal costs, and then just letting the property go. I would never have seen a dime and would be out $17,000. Things can go that way sometimes.

Editor: Is there anything else you want to say about this case study?

Martin Saenz: Yes, this is another good example of why I say it's important to work with a portfolio of notes, and not just one at a time. You need to purchase a group in order to see how you can really profit and excel in this industry. If I had purchased just this one note and then waited the 16 months for resolution, and let's say my legal costs had been doubled because he never came to the table, and he didn't have the money for the early discounted payoff, my takeaway from that experience would be that it was a year and a half later and I was out $17,000.

The lesson I would have learned would be that this industry is horrific. But with a group of five notes, you're able to work and weave your way through the process and it balances out. That's how you really grow in this industry.